GUIDANCE FOR STUDENTS WITH DISABILITIES

GUIDANCE FOR STUDENTS WITH DISABILITIES

Second Edition

By

JUDY H. LOMBANA, PH.D.

Professor
Department of Counselor Education
University of North Florida
Jacksonville, Florida

CHARLES C THOMAS • PUBLISHER
Springfield • Illinois • U.S.A.

Published and Distributed Throughout the World by

CHARLES C THOMAS • PUBLISHER
2600 South First Street
Springfield, Illinois 62794-9265

© *1992 by* CHARLES C THOMAS • PUBLISHER

ISBN 0-398-05804-0

Library of Congress Catalog Card Number: 92-11645

First Edition, 1982

With THOMAS BOOKS *careful attention is given to all details of manufacturing
and design. It is the Publisher's desire to present books that are satisfactory as to
their physical qualities and artistic possibilities and appropriate for their particular
use.* THOMAS BOOKS *will be true to those laws of quality that assure a good
name and good will.*

Printed in the United States of America
SC-R-3

11-29-93 - 16 78 619

Library of Congress Cataloging-in-Publication Data

Lombana, Judy H.
    Guidance for students with disabilities / by Judy H. Lombana. —
2nd ed.
        p.   cm.
    Rev. ed. of: Guidance for handicapped students. © 1982.
    Includes bibliographical references (p.   ) and index.
    ISBN 0-398-05804-0
    1. Handicapped children—Education—United States. 2. Personnel
service in education—United States. I. Lombana, Judy H. Guidance
for handicapped students. II. Title.
LC4031.L64   1992
371.91'0973—dc20   92-11645
                                                            CIP

This book is dedicated to the memory of my grandmother, Anna French Harris, who modeled joyful living regardless of circumstance.

PREFACE

When the first edition of this book was published in 1982, I opened the preface by stating that **The Education for All Handicapped Children Act** may be the most pervasive piece of legislation to affect public school education in this country. I further stated that school counselors had assumed primary responsibility for numerous functions mandated by the legislation, in spite of a lack of appropriate training materials and resources.

The past decade has brought many changes in the education of students with disabilities, but several situations remain the same. At this point, Public Law 94-142 is bolstered by additional legislation and remains the single most pervasive and encompassing federal mandate to impact public school education. Counselors are even more involved in the process now than they were ten years earlier. Unfortunately, training materials and supportive resources for counselors remain scarce.

Guidance for Students with Disabilities is the second edition of a comprehensive and broad-based text that is designed for use at both pre-service and in-service levels. Counselor educators will find the material to parallel traditional discussions of school guidance, while encompassing a current examination of research in various aspects of services for students with disabilities. School counselors will benefit from information that is practical and specific. The topics addressed throughout the text have been developed from those identified by counselors themselves as being areas of greatest need.

Guidance for Students with Disabilities focuses on information for elementary and secondary counselors to increase understanding and skills in working with disabled students. Concerted efforts have been made to avoid duplicating information presented in other guidance texts. Thus, discussions of counseling theory, historical overviews of guidance, and professional affiliations have been purposefully omitted.

Each chapter of **Guidance for Students with Disabilities** provides information that is of direct relevance and practical use to school counselors and counselors-in-training. Chapter 1 includes an overview of special education legislation, with emphasis on sections most directly related to guidance. The counselor's changing roles with disabled students are discussed in reference to the legislation and student needs.

Chapters 2 and 3 are designed to introduce the counselor to various aspects of disability and to examine one important function, fostering positive attitudes toward students with disabilities. The psychological and social ramifications of different types of disability are presented, including the importance of adjustment, parental response, and peer relationships.

Chapters 4, 5, and 6 include discussions of the counselor's role in working directly with disabled students. The needs and characteristics of students that dictate special counseling, career development, and testing approaches are presented; additionally, alternative strategies and instruments that have proven successful with disabled students are discussed.

Chapters 7 and 8 are concerned with guidance functions directed toward significant adults in the lives of students with disabilities: their parents and their teachers. Counselor roles with these significant adults are examined from a consultation and collaboration framework, and several specific guidance services needed by parents and teachers are detailed.

Limitations of language and space constraints invariably lead to certain compromises within texts. One such compromise in this book involves labels. Although the potential dangers of labeling students are addressed throughout the text, the necessity of classification for organizational purposes dictated the use of labels in describing students. Language limitations also led to compromise in conjunction with the use of terms such as **disability** and **handicap.** I have previously applauded the trend toward the disuse of either term as an adjective (Lombana, 1989) and, in fact, this text has been retitled to avoid this situation. However, consistency in the use of terminology is difficult. Most legislation and other legal documentation continues to use established terminology. Further, repeated use of the same phrase can become linguistically awkward. In this text then, terms such as **students with disabilities** are used instead of **disabled students** except when phrasing would be unwieldy or repetitive. Because of the often pejorative implication of the term **handicap,** that word is used with much less frequency than **disability.**

The underlying message of this text is that school guidance services are vital for many disabled youth. It is my hope that the information and strategies presented here will enable school counselors and counselors-in-training to facilitate the personal, educational, and vocational development of students with disabilities.

CONTENTS

GUIDANCE FOR STUDENTS
WITH DISABILITIES

Chapter One

STUDENTS WITH DISABILITIES
AND THE GUIDANCE PROGRAM

Who are the beneficiaries of school guidance programs? For whom are values clarification strategies, classroom guidance activities, small-group counseling, or parent education programs designed? Traditional responses to such queries range from the glib "Guidance is for **everyone**" to the presumptuous "Guidance is for **normal** students with the usual **developmental concerns.**"

Both responses leave volumes unsaid. Can guidance be for **everyone** when counselor/student ratios remain untenable, when the majority of students in large suburban high schools don't even know their counselor's name? Is guidance **really** for everyone? Is it for the young drug user or potential drop-out? Is it for the student with a mental or physical handicap? Reams of reports of actual guidance practices strongly suggest that guidance is **not** for everyone. Furthermore, personnel, financial, and physical constraints are such that guidance probably never will be for everyone.

Guidance as a means to facilitate the developmental process of **normal** youngsters is a long-held and well-cherished tradition. The slogan was undoubtedly conceived to reassure administrators and parents that school counselors were not intending to dabble in long-term psychotherapy with seriously disturbed individuals. Until recent years, the two seemingly disparate views—**guidance for everyone** and **guidance for normal children**—were, in fact, virtually synonymous. The so-called **normal** student comprised the totality of the student body in schools that employed counselors, and the counselors were charged with being available to all.

Social and economic changes have rapidly altered the statistics concerning public school enrollment. For the first time in history, significant numbers of disabled youth are being educated with their nondisabled peers in regular classrooms for all or part of the school day. The impact of this move has been felt by virtually everyone within the educational community. Volumes have been written on ways to adapt curricula or classroom environments to the needs of children with particular handicaps. School systems throughout the country have developed complex and comprehensive procedures for processing exceptional students into the **least restrictive environment**. Parents have become increasingly vocal concerning their legal rights regarding the education of their children with disabilities.

The challenges that school counselors face regarding guidance of students with disabilities are multifaceted. Counselors have been inadequately trained to provide guidance programs for students with handicaps (Lombana, 1980; Tucker, Shepard, & Hurst, 1986). Counselors are not generally knowledgeable about various handicapping conditions; neither are they familiar with the psychological implications of a handicap for the student and his or her family. Beginning counselors are not usually familiar with the various aspects of PL 94-142 (the Education for All Handicapped Children Act) and related legislation.

Although the influx of students with disabilities raises many questions of counselors and poses an unparalleled challenge, the concept of **mainstreaming** also presents potentially exciting opportunities for counselors. They have the satisfaction of providing needed services to a group that has been woefully neglected, both educationally and therapeutically. Counselors have opportunities to renew communication skills with different populations. They have another chance to make meaningful changes within the school environment.

Prior to examining various guidance techniques in conjunction with exceptional students, counselors need to develop several basic understandings. First, they need to become familiar with the legislative history that led to the concept of mainstreaming, as well as the various provisions of major statutes concerning the educational rights of handicapped individuals. Second, counselors need to be able to examine guidance history in the context of counselor role and to begin the formulation of a role definition that is compatible with the training, experience, and functions of counselors who work with students with handicaps.

MAINSTREAMING AND
SPECIAL EDUCATION LEGISLATION

With the passage and implementation of PL 94-142, the Education for All Handicapped Children Act, a quiet revolution that had consumed the better part of a decade came to an end (Abeson & Zettel, 1977). Initiated and led by parents of children with disabilities and furthered through various court decisions, the results of the quiet revolution have radically changed numerous unspoken assumptions regarding society's interactions with individuals with disabilities.

The primary component of the various social struggles, court decisions, and legislative mandates is the concept of mainstreaming. Like most controversial ideas, mainstreaming has been characterized by misunderstandings and stereotypical responses. In an attempt to avoid simplistic approaches to the concept of mainstreaming, a comprehensive definition was adopted by the Council for Exceptional Children at its 1976 National Convention (Baker, 1976):

> Mainstreaming is a belief which involves an educational placement procedure and process for exceptional children based on the conviction that each child should be educated in the least restrictive environment in which the education and related needs can be satisfactorily provided. This concept recognizes that exceptional children have a wide range of special needs, varying greatly in intensity and duration; that there is a recognized continuum of educational settings which may at any given time be appropriate for an individual child's needs; that to the maximum extent appropriate, exceptional children should be educated with non -exceptional children; and that special classes, separate schooling or other removal of an exceptional child from education with non-exceptional children should occur only when the intensity of the child's special education and related needs is such that they cannot be satisfied in an environment including non-exceptional children, even with the provision of supplementary aids and services (pp. 5–7).

In order to further clarify the issues and reassure skeptics, Turnbull and Schulz (1979) discussed what mainstreaming is **not**:

- Mainstreaming is not the wholesale elimination of special education self-contained classes. It does not mean that all handicapped students will be placed in regular classes. Further, it does not automatically imply that those handicapped students who are placed in regular classes will be in that setting for the entire school day.
- Total mainstreaming is not an arrangement that can be accomplished overnight in a school system. Instant change often leads to threatening and unstable classroom environments.
- Mainstreaming is not just the physical presence of a handicapped student in the regular class.
- Mainstreaming does not mean that the placement of handicapped

students in regular classes creates jeopardy for the academic progress of nonhandicapped students.

- Mainstreaming does not mean that the total responsibility for the
  education of handicapped students placed in regular classes will
  fall to the regular class teacher.
- Mainstreaming does not mean putting educators **out on a limb** and
  expecting them to accomplish tasks for which they are not prepared
  (pp. 52–53).

The majority of students with disabilities are able to be fully integrated into regular classes, although some may require supportive services or individualized instructional techniques. Progressively smaller
numbers of students will require the most specialized services. Decision
making must be made with the individual student's needs always in the
forefront; the widest possible array of information from various viewpoints must be incorporated into the decision-making process. At the
same time, the system must be flexible. Constant monitoring, evaluation,
and review must be conducted in order to insure that every student can
move back and forth within the system as circumstances and personal
needs dictate.

The mainstreaming concept evolved over a period of years as a response to a number of different societal conditions and needs. Research
and case studies have repeatedly shown that students themselves **prefer**
to be educated in the regular classroom. Although results have been
mixed, there does appear to be significant evidence to suggest that most
exceptional students perform better, both academically and socially, in
the regular classroom. It is well known that emotional and personality
development of children with disabilities is facilitated when they are
allowed to share as many normal life experiences as possible.

Another potent reason for mainstreaming has been to counteract the
detrimental effects of labeling. Labeling has truly been a double-edged
sword. It has allowed large numbers of students with handicaps to be
identified and educated, and it has often proven necessary in order to
obtain financial support. However, labeling has often led to increased
segregation and has sometimes resulted in social problems more severe
than the identified handicap. The ultimate success of mainstreaming for
students with disabilities appears to be related to several crucial factors:

- **PROFESSIONAL PREPARATION.** Counselors are not well prepared for the many tasks they are expected to undertake. In-service

training to help understand and meet the needs of students with disabilities needs to be a high priority for counselors.

- **MODELS FOR IMPLEMENTATION.** Social isolation and/or rejection is often considered to be the primary barrier to mainstreaming. Studies of children's prejudice toward their handicapped peers reveal that rejection begins early and occurs even when labels, per se, are not an issue. Prejudice toward the people with disabilities is not characteristic of children only. Principals, teachers, counselors, and other educational staff are often anxious about their lack of experience with students with disabilities and may avoid interaction with them.

- **THE NATURE AND EXTENT OF SUPPORT SERVICES.** The concept of mainstreaming mandates that support services such as counseling be made available when needed. Students with disabilities often need counseling for personal concerns; appropriate education involves the student's personal, social, and career development as well as academic achievement. Despite these well-known facts, adequate support services have not been provided in most school systems.

Historical Development of Special Education Legislation

PL 94-142 and related state and federal legislation represent outstanding examples of the **power of the people.** Due to multifaceted efforts of thousands of parents of children with disabilities, certain cases were taken to court, their results were well publicized, and efforts were made to create massive and revolutionary legislation concerned with the educational and civil rights of people with handicaps. Parent organizations have been increasingly active since the formation of United Cerebral Palsy in 1945. The initial thrust was to establish camps and special centers for disabled children and to establish grants and scholarships to further the training of teachers for the handicapped. School systems were often totally unresponsive to parents' requests for educational provisions for their children. If it was arbitrarily determined that a child could not profit from an education or if public transportation was not easily available, denial of services was considered legitimate in some jurisdictions (Abeson & Zettel, 1977). Frustrated parents began turning to the courts for recognition and justice.

Two civil rights cases are often cited among landmark litigation concerning the rights of students. The first, **Brown v. the Board of Education** (1954), resulted in the famous Supreme Court decision that all children are constitutionally entitled to an equal educational opportunity. Although this case dealt primarily with the civil and educational rights of minority students and paved the way for school desegregation, it also served as a major precedent for the educational rights of students with disabilities. The extension of impact of the **Brown v. Board of Education** decision is illustrated by its proclamation that "In these days it is doubtful that any child may reasonably be expected to succeed in life if he is denied the opportunity for an education. Such an opportunity, where the state has undertaken to provide it, is a right which must be made available to all on equal terms (745. Ct. 686, 98L. Ed. 873).

In the middle 1960s another suit on behalf of minority students served to further extend rights to the handicapped. **Hobson v. Hansen** (1967) was a successful challenge to the testing and tracking procedures currently in use. The suit was brought on behalf of black students in Washington, D.C., who claimed to be victims of numerous civil rights violations. The outcome provided the impetus to reorganize tracking systems and to dispense with the use of group intelligence tests as sole criteria for placements in certain tracks.

Landmark litigation directly concerned with handicapped student education includes two cases in the early 1970s. In 1971, the Pennsylvania Association for Retarded Children (PARC) successfully sued the State of Pennsylvania for failure to provide all retarded children with a publicly supported education. In 1972, a similar suit, **Mills v. Board of Education of the District Columbia**, was filed on behalf of all children denied admittance to public schools. The Mills decision extended the rights of retarded children to include students with **any** handicap. The message communicated through both cases was essentially the same: no child is uneducable, and states have the responsibility to provide free and appropriate education to all.

Public Law 94-142

The **Education for all Handicapped Children Act** is often referred to as the "bill of rights for the handicapped." It represents the culmination of numerous significant judicial decisions and thousands of days of legislative effort by parents of children with disabilities. The law is unusual in its specificity and comprehensiveness: it leaves little room for interpretation.

PL 94-142 was passed overwhelmingly by Congress and was signed into law by President Ford in November 1975. Full implementation of the legislation occurred in September 1978.

The overall intent of the law is reflected in its introductory statement: "It is the purpose of this Act to assure that all handicapped children have available to them, within the time periods specified, . . . a free appropriate public education which emphasizes special education and related services designed to meet their unique need . . . " (Public Law 94-142, 1975, Sec. 3, c.).

PL 94-142 applies to all children with disabilities and youth, ages 3 to 21 inclusive. For the purposes of the Act, children with disabilities are defined as those who are "mentally retarded, hard of hearing, deaf, orthopedically impaired, other health impaired, speech impaired, visually handicapped, seriously emotionally disturbed, or children with specific learning disabilities who by reason thereof require special education and related services" (Sec. 4(a) (1)).

Among the major accomplishments of PL 94-142 are the following:

- It establishes major and extensive identification procedures.
- It provides assurance of full service for education of students with disabilities, with a detailed timetable.
- It guarantees due process procedures for students with disabilities and their families.
- It provides for extensive school/home consultation.
- It requires extensive in-service training to be provided for school personnel.
- It mandates public education in the least restrictive environment.
- It makes provisions for nondiscriminatory testing.
- It specifies policies and procedures that guarantee confidentiality of data and information.
- It mandates the development and implementation of an Individualized Educational Program (IEP) for each student with a disability.
- It provides for a free and appropriate education for students with handicaps.
- It provides a surrogate to act for any student whose parents or guardians are unknown or unavailable.

While virtually all of these provisions have implications for school counselors and guidance programs, several components or concepts inherent in the law are particularly important for an understanding of the statute's far-reaching intent.

Zero Reject

Essentially, this principle declares that no child with a disability can be excluded from a free and appropriate public school education. Rather than mere admittance to educational programs, zero reject principles mandate that services and instruction be suited in every way to the student's handicapping condition and to his or her individual needs.

Least Restrictive Placement

The concept of **least restrictive environment** is often erroneously considered to be synonymous with **mainstreaming.** In point of fact, mainstreaming is not mentioned in PL 94-142, and the law is specific in its mandate that a child be educated in the setting that is least restrictive for him or her. For many students with disabilities, the **least restrictive environment** would include the regular classroom for all or part of a school day. For other children, however, mainstreaming would in fact be **very** restrictive in terms of its impact on a child's educational and social attainment. In these instances, a self-contained classroom would be less restrictive in terms of meeting the child's individual needs.

The Individualized Education Program (IEP)

One of the most potent aspects of PL 94-142 is its emphasis on the Individualized Educational Program (IEP), which must be developed for every child who is identified as handicapped, regardless of placement. The IEP has become the focal point of due process, program monitoring, and educational service (Stowitschek & Kelso, 1989). Although there is no standard format for IEPs, each must contain specific information, including the following:

- A statement of the student's present levels of educational performance.
- A statement of annual goals, including short-term instructional objectives.
- A statement of the specific educational services to be provided, and the extent to which the student will be able to participate in regular educational programs.
- The projected date for initiation and duration of the services.

- Appropriate objective criteria and evaluation procedures and schedules for determining, on at least an annual basis, whether instructional objectives are being met (Sec. 4(1) (19)).

The plan must be developed as a team effort after careful screening and evaluation procedures have been completed. Parents must be invited to participate in the IEP meeting. Goals, objectives, educational services, and evaluation procedures must be established for each child. The IEP process is necessarily time-consuming and deliberately thorough. In many cases, more than one meeting will be required to develop a plan for a given student, and the plan can be reviewed at any time by parents.

Due Process Requirements and Parental Rights

The due process requirement of PL 94-142 is complex and comprehensive. It is designed to involve the handicapped child's parent (or guardian) in virtually every aspect of the educational planning process and to provide systematic procedures for arbitration when disagreements exist. The major elements of the due process requirement include the following:

- Parents must give written consent before evaluation of a child can occur.
- Parents must be given the opportunity to participate in all planning meetings concerning the child's educational program and must consent to the program which has been planned.
- Parents must be given opportunities to present complaints concerning the identification, evaluation, or placement of their child.
- Parents have a right to obtain an independent educational evaluation of their child if they disagree with the results of the evaluation conducted through the school system.
- Parents have the right to access to all relevant records concerning their child.
- Parents have the right to an impartial due process hearing and the right to appeal the findings of the hearing. Either the parents or the school can request a hearing whenever disagreements occur.

The due process requirements of the law depend largely on effective communication between school and home in order to be smoothly implemented. Counselors at both elementary and secondary levels are often designated as the individuals who coordinate the various steps in the procedure. This means that the counselor is involved in much correspondence, telephone, and personal contact with parents.

The Comprehensive Evaluation Process

PL 94-142 is relatively specific in terms of the various procedures that must be undertaken in order to properly identify, place, instruct, and monitor the progress of individual students with disabilities. Components of the process that are common to all schools are briefly described as follows; certain aspects of the evaluation procedures, such as individualized testing, are discussed in more detail in other chapters.

Screening

The purpose of **screening** is to identify certain children who exhibit some characteristics associated with a particular handicap. Screening is often routinely conducted for the purpose of identifying children with vision, hearing, or other health problems. Increasingly, young children are screened for learning disabilities or mental retardation as well. The counselor is usually involved in the screening process through scheduling physical tests, administering certain devices, and/or preparing necessary paperwork. Techniques and instruments used in screening are discussed in Chapter 6.

Referral

Whether the screening process consists of a standardized measure such as a group intelligence test or an informal procedure such as a teacher-made test or classroom observation, certain children will be referred for further assessment. Often, the referral is made from the classroom teacher to the counselor; sometimes the child's parents will initiate the referral. Most school systems have developed forms or checklists in an attempt to objectify the referral procedure and to provide as much information as possible. The teacher may be expected to describe the child's behavior or condition in detail, to submit samples of the child's work, or to record scores of screening instruments and other available measures. The counselor and teacher are usually in contact regarding the child's situation prior to the submission of a formal referral. The counselor may have observed the child in the classroom, contacted the parents for information, or helped the teacher compile the necessary referral information.

Parental Consent

The importance of keeping parents informed and the necessity for obtaining their consent throughout the evaluation process cannot be overemphasized. Although permission for screening is not required because it is considered an educational procedure appropriate for **all** students, any action taken on behalf of an individual student should be accomplished only with parental approval. Most school districts have developed standard forms for parental consent, but such forms have not always been legitimate. Efforts must be made to insure that parents fully understand and agree to the actions that are to be taken for their child. This means that all communication must be in the parents' native language or preferred mode of communication (in the event that a parent is deaf or blind).

Most counselors have found that the ease of obtaining parental consent is often directly related to the care that school personnel have taken to communicate effectively. A telephone call or personalized note that explains the assessment procedure in terms of the individual student's needs will help insure speedy return of parental permission forms. A parent conference may be warranted in some instances. The important point is to **involve** the parents and help them contribute to the evaluation process.

Assessment

After parental consent has been received, individual, multifactored assessment of the child is undertaken in an effort to more clearly ascertain the nature and extent of the suspected problem and to provide data for instruction and related services. The assessment process is often complex for children with disabilities; those procedures are the primary focus of Chapter 6.

IEP Committee Meeting

Following completion of formal and informal assessment of an individual student, a committee must meet for the purpose of reviewing assessment results, determining the services that the student needs and selecting the least restrictive placement. The counselor usually serves on the committee and often acts as the coordinator. Others involved may include the parents, the classroom teacher, the school psychologist, and a

special education teacher. Often, other specialists such as a speech therapist are included and, in some cases, the student will participate.

Parental Agreement

While the parents are invited to participate in the IEP meeting (often
called a **staffing** or **child study**), they are not required to do so. The
parents' concurrence with the findings and recommendations of the
committee **are** required and must be recorded in writing. If parents
disagree with the findings and recommendations concerning their child,
they may institute due process procedures.

IEP Development

The next step is to outline the specifications of the IEP, including the
instructional area(s) involved, related services such as counseling, duration of services, goals, objectives, strategies, and evaluation plan.

Delivery of Services

The IEP, including related services, is then implemented with a
designated monitoring process instituted. The various guidance services
discussed throughout the text are included here.

Annual Review

An annual inventory of the student's progress in relation to the IEP is
required by PL 94-142. Although additional assessment is required only
every three years, an annual review of the child's progress helps to
update information and provide for needed changes in placement or
services.

THE COUNSELOR AND STUDENTS WITH DISABILITIES

Until recently, literature dealing with the school counselor's role with
students with disabilities was virtually nonexistent. In spite of longstanding guidance commitments to serve **all** students, a sizable portion
of the population was obviously being ignored. In search of an explanation,
Wyne and Skjei (1970) suggested that most counselors did not consider
themselves responsible for certain categories of students. Instead, counselors rationalized that since special education teachers were more familiar with the students' problems, the teachers should provide counseling.
Such negative and delimiting attitudes represented the prevailing

educational mood at the time and led to some current problems within the profession. Despite public statements concerning the counselor's professional commitment to recognize and facilitate the potential for growth and self-fulfillment in all students, counselors reacted in much the same way as regular classroom teachers and administrators. Everyone wished the best for students with disabilities—but no one was willing to assume any responsibility for them.

Guidance Functions for Students with Disabilities

In general, counselor roles with children with disabilities are not perceived to differ from those functions performed with any other students. The primary services—group counseling, individual counseling, staff consultation, coordination of services, testing and evaluation—can be found in virtually all counselor role statements and are the main topics considered in most school-oriented counselor education programs. However, a closer look at the literature and actual practice reveals some significant differences:

- **CLASSROOM GUIDANCE.** Psychological education, affective education, or other interchangeable terms used to describe classroom guidance activities usually focus on developmental topics such as values clarification, moral development, or decision making. While these areas are mentioned in the special education literature, the most frequent and pervasive plea is for activities designed to foster positive attitudes toward students with disabilities. This focus represents a significant departure from typical counselor function.
- **CONSULTATION WITH TEACHERS.** Generally, counselors are urged to consult with teachers on topics such as improving communication strategies or modifying children's classroom misbehavior. In addition, teachers need help in dealing with their resentment toward having students with disabilities in their classes, and they need to work through their own anxieties concerning handicaps.
- **CONSULTATION WITH PARENTS.** The literature on parent consultation generally focuses on parent-child interaction; counselors are encouraged to assume an active role in helping parents learn communication techniques that facilitate relationship building. In addition to such developmental activities, the counselor's role with parents of students with disabilities is broadened to include a num-

ber of very different activities. The counselor is urged to help parents overcome guilt concerning their child's disability, to foster the parents' acceptance of the child, to organize parent support groups, and to provide parents with materials and information relative to their child's disability.

- **COUNSELING WITH STUDENTS.** Guidance literature and training programs generally advocate personal growth as the primary topic for group counseling sessions. Individual counseling is usually perceived as being more problem-oriented, with most issues involving peer relationships, parental communication problems, or school-related concerns. Counselors are often urged to employ a nondirective approach that provides ample opportunity for verbal expression, exploration of feelings, and insight. In counseling students with handicaps, however, the focus is often quite different. Although other procedures may be advocated for students with certain disabilities, the focus may need to be on a concrete, activity-oriented counseling approach such as role playing or art therapy. The overwhelming counseling concern of students with disabilities is poor self-concept, and counselors should use all possible means of providing emotional support.

- **ASSESSMENT.** Counselors traditionally administer or supervise the administration of standardized tests of achievement, aptitude, and vocational interest. Frequently, the same instruments are used over a period of years so that test administration becomes primarily a clerical chore. When students with disabilities are involved, however, testing takes on an entirely different cast. The counselor will need to become familiar with the various tests used for screening and identification for each handicapping condition. New knowledge will be required concerning modifications of standardized instruments for blind, deaf, and other disabled people. Conditions and procedures for test administration are different and will require new knowledge and skills by the counselor.

- **COORDINATION OF SERVICES.** Whereas counselors' traditional coordinating functions have frequently involved perfunctory tasks such as scheduling psychological evaluations, new demands are emerging. Many counselors have assumed the responsibility of coordinating the total placement process; others have found themselves serving as liaison between regular teachers, parents, and resource teachers for every educational decision concerning the handicapped student.

The counselor's functions with students with disabilities appear to extend considerably beyond those with other students. In every area, the counselor is expected to perform the same tasks with students with handicaps as with the nonhandicapped. Apart from these functions, however, is an array of tasks, activities, and responsibilities that are specific to the needs of disabled youth. These tasks necessarily involve new knowledge and additional skills; in most cases, the responsibilities are so different and so complex that they signify a drastic role change.

Counselor Preparation and Professional Development

One logical and justifiable reason for not working with students with handicaps is the fact that it has only been during the past few years that systematic efforts have been undertaken to determine how inadequate their education has been and what types of training are needed by counselors. In the first study of its kind, Lebsock and DeBlassie (1975) surveyed several hundred school counselors in the midwestern United States, as well as 65 university counselor education departments throughout the country. The researchers were interested in determining the scope of services provided to students with handicaps, counselors' perceptions of their own competence in working with handicapped youth, the extent to which counselors received special education training, and whether or not counselor educators were attempting to train counselors to work with exceptional students.

Among the counselor education departments surveyed, only 13% required graduate students to complete one or more special education courses. Only 55% of the counselor education respondents indicated that they prepare and encourage their graduates to work with special education students, although 87% stated that counselors **should** serve handicapped youth. Among the counselors surveyed, approximately 43% had taken **no** special education courses.

In a survey of Florida school counselors (Lombana, 1980), the gap between training and practice was vividly illustrated. Although counselors were spending a disproportionate amount of time with students with disabilities considering their relatively small numbers, virtually all counselor training (both in-service and pre-service) had been in areas unrelated to students with handicaps.

Of the counselors in the Florida survey, 57% reported no university coursework in special education, and there were indications that actual figures are much higher. Statistics concerning in-service education were even more startling: 35% of the counselors had received no in-service, and there was considerable disparity between counselor functions and types of training received. For example, **screening** was indicated as the most frequently conducted activity with students with disabilities, named by 67% of the respondents. However, only 6% had received inservice training in screening procedures. Five years later, another researcher (Lusk, 1985) surveyed 91 high school counselors regarding their work with exceptional students. The results revealed that the majority of respondents were not working with significant numbers of special education students. Almost one-half of the counselors indicated they would not be interested in taking special education coursework to increase their effectiveness in working with these students.

In view of the extension of services required by students with handicaps and the lack of knowledge expressed by counselors who work with them, it is critical that training, whether it be pre-service or in-service, be provided for school counselors. The remainder of this text has been designed to assist in this training effort.

Chapter Two

UNDERSTANDING STUDENTS
WITH DISABILITIES

Counselors and other school staff often shy away from personal involvement with students with handicaps. When asked, counselors are likely to report that they know so little about specific handicaps that they cannot help disabled students. Counselors, like other professionals, tend to view students with disabilities as essentially different from others; this perceived difference creates a psychological barrier that is extremely difficult to overcome.

The barrier of misunderstanding between the disabled and the able-bodied is perceived even more strongly by students with disabilities themselves. The desire to be understood is perhaps the greatest of the various special needs of disabled people; it is ironic that such a pervasive and important need is also one that is almost totally beyond the individual disabled person's control. Mystery, fear, and misconceptions abound and obscure the humanness and essential sameness that all persons share.

Educators will never be effective teachers, counselors, or consultants to students with disabilities as long as the barriers of misunderstanding exist. Neither will they be able to implement programs designed to foster acceptance and positive attitudes among other students in the school under these conditions. Understanding students with disabilities involves three major learnings:

- Each handicapped student has a singular and unique personality, which serves to differentiate that student from all others. Yet, each student shares basic human needs with all of humanity.
- Certain differences between disabled and nondisabled people do serve to differentiate the groups in general terms. These differences are not brought about as a direct result of a disability, but rather by societal expectations, reactions, and opinions regarding the disability.
- Specific aspects of a given disability, whether medically or devel-

opmentally oriented, may alter the way in which a person must operate within the environment. Each individual calls upon personal and unique strengths, coping mechanisms, and other characteristics.

Students with handicaps are, first and foremost, individuals. Literature concerned with relationship of disability to personality has shown little evidence to support the notion that various disabilities are associated with particular types of personality. In fact, basic personality structure appears to be exceptionally stable, even in the face of serious somatic change.

While individuality and uniqueness must be the foremost consideration when attempting to understand and relate to an individual student, it would be erroneous to assume that disability has **no** impact on personality. The relationship between physical disability and psychological impairment is not simple, and individual reactions to disability are wide-ranging. Some of the more consistent differences include the following:

- Physically handicapped students are generally less mature than their nonhandicapped age-mates.
- People with physical handicaps have more problems with social relationships than do nondisabled persons.
- Children with disabilities experience greater feelings of anxiety, conflict, and defensiveness than nonhandicapped children.
- The suicide rate is higher for people with physical handicaps than for the general population.
- Children with disabilities are more inhibited than are nonhandicapped youngsters.

The factors that operate to create differences between handicapped and nonhandicapped persons are not always predictable. There do appear to be greater personality differences between disabled and nondisabled people than between representatives of various types of disability. This finding adds credence to the notion that in terms of behavior patterns, the **fact** of impairment is more significant than the **type**. Another finding that appears to be fairly consistent through various research efforts is that persons with mild impairment are more likely to be socially or behaviorally maladjusted than those who are more severely disabled.

SOCIETAL EXPECTATIONS AND PEOPLE WITH DISABILITIES

Disability has been defined as a "social value judgment" and it is undoubtedly true that most types of physical deviance are viewed quite differently in various cultures. Among the Choco Indians of Panama, for example, it would certainly be a handicap to be a twin; such **abnormalities** are considered evil and are put to death. In some societies, persons with epilepsy are isolated and overtly shunned or even killed because of their **curse;** in other cultures they are venerated and exalted due to their **spiritual gift.**

Within our own society, the effects of societal expectations of behavior can be viewed within all socioeconomic strata and in a variety of situations. Studies have shown that teachers have higher academic expectations and greater liking for pretty girls than for unattractive boys. Even a person's **name** evokes consistent responses, with students named David, Michael, Ann, or Jennifer achieving a significantly more favorable response than children who are named Herman, Eloise, Dorothy, or Edgar.

Social expectations, then, create environmental situations to which handicapped people must respond. These expectations result in certain behaviors which, in turn, create further expectations. Thus, a chicken/egg dilemma is born and continually fostered. The end result is, all too often, a negative self-evaluation by the disabled student.

Interactions with Others

The self-concept is largely created through interactions with others. Through shared experiences, verbal feedback, and subtle facial and postural clues, an individual begins to form an impression of what he or she is about. People quickly learn if they are perceived as cheerful, bright, selfish, or shy. Even three- and four-year-old children are able to discern that societal requirements for **pretty** include curly rather than lank hair and symmetrical rather than asymmetrical features. Likewise, disabled people learn their roles quickly and can play them well. Blind people learn to be passive and unassuming; deaf persons learn to be suspicious and rigid; students with learning disabilities become adept at failing and acting out in class.

Many students with handicaps have very limited interactions with nondisabled people other than their families. Thus, they may not learn a variety of responses and feedback mechanisms from which they can choose to assimilate. Those students fortunate enough to have been surrounded by accepting and supportive adults who refuse to view the disabled child as **different** generally grow up to view themselves positively.

The Effects of Labeling

Labeling, in whatever form, generally results in the reduction of individuality and the building of a stereotypic characterization. Labels whether positive (a **gifted** child; a **super-jock**) or negative (**retard, cripple**) carry with them certain behavioral expectations that are extremely difficult to escape. Labels help create behavioral problems and further societal stereotypes regardless of their form or intent. Most damaging in the short run are those cruel names generally invented by children to express their fear of certain behavioral or physical differences, such as **dummy, sickie, wacko, gimp.** Many common expressions, recognized and used throughout our society to convey certain ideas, serve to perpetuate negative opinions and increase the inferior status of handicapped persons. Examples of these damaging expressions include **blind as a bat, deaf and dumb, lamebrain,** and **thick-headed.**

Professionals, too, contribute to the damaging effects of labeling. All too often professionals refer to **the blind, a paraplegic,** or **retardates,** as if those persons shared commonalities beyond the fact of their specific disability. Although considerable progress has been made in recent years in terms of eliminating certain distasteful terms (people who are mentally retarded are seldom classified as **idiots, morons, or imbeciles** anymore), the professional literature still occasionally makes reference to disabled persons in condescending or patronizing terms.

Labeling for the purpose of educational classification may be necessary; however, numerous research efforts have shown that both children and adults respond stereotypically to labels.

While the total elimination of labels in education and rehabilitation is unlikely, professionals can work to reduce their negative impact on students with handicaps. Using labels properly is one way that stereotypes can be combated.

ADJUSTMENT TO DISABILITY

All disabled persons must come to some terms with their disability. The person who is able to fully accept the disability will be the one who views it as one aspect, but only one, of his or her life. Others may not be so successful in the adjustment process; for these people, the disability will assume a more significant role in their lives and will probably have more negative effects on self-concept and interpersonal relationships.

The adjustment process is as unique as the individual person. However, there are several conditions that, for most people, help predict the nature and the degree of adjustment. Some of the more influential determinants include age of onset of the disability, severity of the handicap, and the personality of the individual.

Age at Onset

Generally speaking, the earlier a person becomes disabled, the less traumatic is the adjustment process. Thus, a person who is born blind is likely to undergo a far less stressful adjustment than would an adult who is suddenly blinded through disease or accident. Of course, there are life stages during which acceptance of a disability, or any other perceived limitation, is particularly difficult. Even for persons who were congenitally disabled and have adjusted to the limitations imposed by the handicap, adolescence is a time of particular stress.

To a large extent, the manner in which an individual copes with adventitious disability is determined by his or her characteristic way of adjusting to other stressful situations. The individual who is basically self-sufficient, optimistic, and goal-oriented will generally have a more successful adjustment to a handicap than will a person who, prior to becoming disabled, was generally dependent, apathetic, or morose. For students whose disability involves an overt physical alteration such as amputation or spinal cord injury, adjustment may be determined by the individual's **body** image. The body image includes not only the individual's personal investment in his or her body but also the views and values of other significant people and culture at large. People who strongly value certain bodily aspects such as physical strength, facial beauty, or agility may have a particularly difficult time adjusting if their disability involves a loss of their valued traits.

Parental Reactions

Parents of disabled children exert a profound influence on the adjustment of their child to his or her condition. Parents undergo the same stages in the adjustment process as do their children; in fact, parents are forced to undergo two distinct but interrelated processes. They must cope with their own adjustment to their child's handicap, and they must help the child come to terms with it.

Whereas a child who is congenitally disabled suffers considerably less trauma than the adolescent who suddenly becomes handicapped, parents suffer far more if the child is born with a handicap or acquires it very early in life. In these instances, parents invariably experience the more painful aspects of the mourning process-denial, shock, grief, guilt, depression-as they grieve for their **lost, perfect** child. Because the bonds of parental love and support are fragile at this early stage, rejection or overprotection is more likely to occur. When a child is handicapped later, such as during adolescence, parents are able to more readily accept their **loss** and can concentrate on helping the child cope with the trauma.

The Process of Adjustment

It has been observed that most people, particularly those who are adventitiously handicapped, progress through a series of stages in the process adjusting to their disability. The process is often likened to the mourning or grief cycle as popularized by Kubler-Ross (1975). The stages of adjustment are similar, but various writers have described them in different terms, so that there is no universally accepted portrayal of the adjustment process.

Denial

When a person first experiences a shock such as a sudden disability, he or she may not be emotionally prepared to accept the reality and the implications of the disability. Denial is a psychological protection against overwhelming threat and is, therefore, therapeutic. Generally, denial lasts from a few days to several weeks, and it allows the individual to gradually face the fact of the disability. Denial is usually most obvious in adventitiously disabled people and in those in whom the disability was sudden rather than progressive. Because denial usually occurs immediately following a disability, a period in which the individual is often hospitalized, school counselors, teachers, and other educational staff may seldom encounter students in this stage. There are instances, of course, in which people continue to deny their disability to such a degree that it interferes with rehabilitation or psychological adjustment.

Mourning

As a person moves out of the denial stage and begins to acknowledge the fact of a disability, he or she will almost invariably experience a mourning period. Anxiety, worry, depression, and hostility are all characteristic expressions of mourning, and an individual may experience any one or all of these reactions.

Although anxiety and outwardly directed anger are common experiences of the mourning period, they are certainly not universal phenomena. While some students may express their frustration and grief by aggressive and hostile behavior, others respond in an opposite manner and become depressed.

Depression is normal and for most people it will pass in time. Some disabled people, however, appear to relish their depression and can develop **learned helplessness** (Seligman, 1975), a situation in which they relinquish total control of their lives. Some depressed people begin a vicious cycle by dwelling on what is depressing them. This, of course, tends to make them more depressed, which makes them worry more.

Acceptance

Most disabled people ultimately garner the emotional strength to concentrate more on their abilities than on their limitations. And thus the stage of **adjustment** is begun, a period that lasts, as it does for everyone, the rest of their lives. During the adjustment stage, which in itself can be painful as a person struggles with the temptation to remain dependent, passive, or hostile, understanding and acceptance are the greatest gifts that counselors and teachers can offer. The process of adjustment can seldom be hurried, and the procedure is likely to be fraught with frustration and regression. The end result, however, can well mean that a person has progressed through a massive trauma, overcome numerous obstacles, and emerged a strong and happy individual.

CHARACTERISTICS OF STUDENTS WITH SPECIFIC DISABILITIES

In order to successfully counsel students with disabilities and collaborate with their teachers and parents, counselors will need to have at least a cursory understanding of the medical, psychological, and social characteristics associated with various handicapping conditions.

Learning Disabilities

Understanding the causes and characteristics associated with learning disabled students is made particularly difficult by the elusive nature of the syndrome. The problems are amply illustrated by the fact that through the years, literally dozens of terms have been bandied about in an attempt to adequately define the problem. Among the more commonly used terms are the following:

attention disordered	emotionally disturbed
behavior disordered	hyperactive
behavior problem	hyperkinetic
brain damaged	interactive child
brain injured	language disabled
conceptually handicapped	minimal brain dysfunction
delayed language	neurologically impaired
developmental aphasic	neurophrenia
disruptive/aggressive	perceptually handicapped
dyslexic	socially maladjusted
educationally disabled	specific reading disability
educationally handicapped	subtle neurological impairment
emotional blockage	Strauss syndrome

The term **learning disability** or **specific learning disability** is probably the most frequently cited name and represents the syndrome as discussed in PL 94-142 and related legislation.

There are almost as many definitions for learning disabilities as there are names for the syndrome. PL 94-142 (Section 4, Part A (3)) refers to learning disabled children as "those children who have a disorder in one or more of the basic psychological processes involved in understanding or in using language, spoken or written, which disorder may manifest itself in imperfect ability to listen, think, speak, read, write, spell, or do mathematical calculations. Such disorders include such conditions as perceptual handicaps, brain injury, minimal brain dysfunction, dyslexia, and developmental aphasia. Such term does not include children who have learning problems which are primarily the result of visual, hearing, or motor handicaps, of mental retardation, of emotional disturbance, or of environmental, cultural or economic disadvantage."

As can be inferred from the lack of specificity in this definition, learning disabilities represent one of the least understood handicapping conditions. Recently, a focus on social skills has been emphasized and experts in the education field generally agree that social skills deficits are among the most prevalent characteristics of students with learning disabilities (Gresham & Elliott, 1989). However, efforts to trace the various causes associated with learning disabilities have met with ambiguous results.

Learning disabilities represent more of a collection of various learning and behavioral difficulties than a single handicapping condition. Thus, it is not surprising that the incidence of learning disability is higher than for all other areas of exceptionality. Currently, 42% of all identified exceptional students are labeled learning disabled (Grolnick & Ryan, 1990). Boys are five to six times more likely than girls to be identified as learning disabled, although in recent years an increasing number of girls have been so labeled.

Academic, Personal, and Social Implications

The one word that most characterizes the learning disabled student's self-perception is **failure.** Failure begins early when the child is unable to avoid the behaviors that displease parents. Distractibility, erratic eating and sleeping habits, hyperactivity, and temper tantrums characterize the early behavior of many learning disabled children, and parents may be unprepared to cope. Problems are compounded by the fact that organic causes may not be evident. Parents quickly learn to expect less of their learning disabled child than of their other children. Increasing evidence (Amerikaner & Omizo, 1984; Coles, 1987; Green, 1989, 1990) support the notion that in many cases the families of learning disabled children exhibit poor parenting skills and are in various ways dysfunctional.

Of course, many parents recognize early that the child's behavior is beyond his or her control and that special efforts and strategies will need to be implemented in order to combat the disability. In some cases, drugs are used to treat hyperactivity and distractibility; special diets have been employed with some success. Most parents have found that, outside of individualized academic instruction, behavioral problems can best be met through the implementation of behavior modification principles within a structured but accepting environment.

At school, the learning disabled student often encounters escalating amounts of failure. The student's inability to remain on task, to remember simple instructions, or to avoid bothering other students can result in a great deal of frustration on the part of the teacher. Teachers learn to deal with learning disabled students by avoiding responding to them and by giving more negative reinforcement than to other students (Kavale, 1988). Students with learning disabilities learn to cope with the classroom environment in their own way: by looking busy, not being disruptive, not getting into trouble, and not working in school. But failure continues to haunt the student, failure that is more poignant because it is often accompanied by the taunts of other students and the sarcasm of the teacher. In many instances students with learning disabilities, particularly boys, adopt a defense that is characterized by hostility and antisocial attitudes, resulting in a vicious cycle of acting out/punishment/failure.

Although learning disabilities per se are considered a relatively minor disability, the failure syndrome and poor self concept that develops can prove to be a major handicap (Chapman, 1988). Early detection and remediation are vital for the prevention of emotional difficulties. Students with learning disabilities must develop skills or talents in an area in which they are not disabled in order to combat the failure identity.

Mental Retardation

Through the years, the field of mental retardation has undergone numerous changes, and it continues to experience rapid growth as medical, psychological, and sociological discoveries are made. Among the more significant and helpful changes are the increasing public awareness and understanding concerning the nature of mental retardation. Parent groups and public figures have been largely responsible for breaking down some of the myths and stereotypical views concerning mental retardation; state and federal legislation, the initiation of special projects such as the Special Olympics, and increased professional emphasis on normalization have all helped develop public awareness of mental retardation.

Although medical and psychological findings concerning mental retardation have increased rapidly in recent years, attitudinal change usually occurs slowly. Therefore, in spite of widely publicized efforts to portray mentally retarded people as worthwhile and productive citizens, negative responses remain. Within the school setting, the counselor can be a force toward assisting mentally retarded students in the process of normalization.

Definitions of Mental Retardation

According to the American Association on Mental Deficiency, mental retardation refers to "significantly subaverage general intellectual functioning existing concurrently with deficits in adaptive behavior, and manifested during the developmental period" (Grossman, 1983, p. 1).

Sub-average intellectual functioning refers to performance on an individual intelligence test that is more than two standard deviations below the test's mean. The **developmental period,** according to the AAMD, refers to the period of time between conception and the end of the 18th year. **Adaptive behavior** includes successful coping with the ordinary events of maturing, including personal self-care, social abilities, vocational independence, and school achievement.

Of particular importance is the emphasis on deficits in adaptive behavior. Many people erroneously assume that the sole criterion or characteristic of mental retardation is a low intelligence quotient. In actuality, if this were the case, approximately 16 percent of the population would be considered to be retarded instead of the current figure of 3 percent.

Degrees of retardation have long been categorized by IQ level, whereas only recently have attempts been made to describe examples of adaptive behavior at different levels. Although categories do overlap and no indication of permanence should be inferred, the various classifications of mental retardation include the following:

- **EDUCABLE MENTALLY HANDICAPPED.** This category includes persons whose IQs generally range from 50 to 75, with maximum mental age of 8 to 12 years. EMH children are usually normal in appearance and are similar to their nonretarded peers in terms of personality variables. They can be expected to succeed in various functional areas of academic learning and, given appropriate assistance, many can be independent economically and vocationally.
- **TRAINABLE MENTALLY HANDICAPPED.** TMH students usually achieve scores of 25 to 50 on standardized individual intelligence tests. Many have significant physical or sensory impairments.

They can learn routine tasks and simple academic skills, and many are vocationally successful in simple assembly-type work. They can achieve some measure of independence in terms of self-help skills.

- **PROFOUNDLY MENTALLY HANDICAPPED.** Profoundly or severely retarded children usually have intelligence quotients below 25. They can often learn personal skills such as toileting, dressing, use of tableware, and some speech. They are almost totally dependent on others for survival and are usually cared for in institutions.

Normalization of Mentally Retarded Persons

The effects of mental retardation on personality characteristics are, as yet, unclear. Retarded children and adults may have limited social opportunities, which in turn leads to shyness and immaturity. Retarded individuals frequently display poor impulse control and demonstrate a lack of "common sense" (Gloeckler & Simpson, 1988). Differences in personality structure are often particularly apparent during adolescence. Retarded youth have difficulty comprehending the physical and emotional changes caused by adolescence, and they are unable to anticipate future changes. Because of their maturing physical structure, adults often expect them to perform beyond their ability, resulting in frustration and feelings of devaluation.

Research and case studies consistently point out the relationship between adaptive behavior and opportunities for normalization. The more that a retarded person perceives that he or she is viewed as normal, the more normal that person can become. Some research has shown that retarded students placed in regular classrooms experienced significant improvement in self concept and academics, while other research has found partial integration to be the most helpful. A recent study (Bak, Cooper, Dobroth, & Siperstein, 1987) showed that students viewed retarded students in self contained classrooms as less capable than those attending resource classes.

From case studies, observation, and research efforts, it becomes increasingly clear that the label **mentally retarded** itself can prompt others to respond to the labeled person in negative ways. Segregated living and learning environments inhibit the development of basic socialization skills, thus augmenting the deficits in adaptive behavior. When children are placed in school or home environments that discourage them from achieving to their fullest potential, the children develop a level of dependence that can prevent them from assuming independent living skills. Mainstreaming, then, is more than an educational concept for retarded students; it is, as well, a form of treatment, a serious attempt to use the social and educational environment as a means of improving the intellectual performance and adaptive behavior of students.

Emotional/Behavioral Disorders

No area of disability is as nebulous and difficult to define as that which is often referred to as **emotional disturbance.** The causes and manifestations are so many and varied that any attempt to find commonalities leads only to superficial and general descriptions.

The difficulty in defining and coping educationally with emotional, social, or behavioral disorders is illustrated by the fact that no fewer than 24 different labels are used for identification purposes within the 50 state departments of education. The most frequent term is **emotionally disturbed,** although **socially maladjusted, behaviorally disordered,** and **socially maladjusted** are used in some states. Two trends are apparent: an increasing emphasis on the word **behavior** in place of **emotional** and a focus on terms delineating **serious** problems (Center, 1989).

The incidence of emotional or behavioral disturbance appears to be rapidly increasing. One potent indicator is the suicide rate; unfortunately, suicides among American youth are increasing by almost epidemic proportions. It is the second leading cause of death among teenagers (Simmons, 1987), and it is estimated that for every suicide, there are 8 to 10 suicide attempts. A recent study of 70 adolescents admitted to a psychiatric hospital (Salzman & Salzman, 1989) revealed that the vast majority had histories of drug use, physical and/or sexual abuse, and school failure. More than one-third had attempted suicide at least once and more than half were diagnosed with clinical depression.

Causes of Behavioral Disturbance

Very little is known regarding the etiology of behavioral or emotional disturbance, although it is widely accepted that a myriad of factors can influence the personality and may result in permanent damage in some people. Seemingly innocuous variables such as intelligence, names and nicknames, and birth order have been shown to be linked with certain personality characteristics, although such variables cannot be used for serious predictive purposes. In some instances, various organic causes can lead to brain damage, which in turn influences personality development.

The circular thinking involved in attempts to define the causes of behavioral disturbance is particularly evident in the role of the family. It is well known that parental responses to a handicap can contribute to difficulties in the child's adjustment and subsequent emotional well-being. However, many authorities assert that in cases in which emotional or behavioral disturbances are the handicapping condition, faulty parenting is often the underlying cause.

While the precise nature of the role of the family in the development of emotional disturbance is unclear, the fact of its influence cannot be denied. While it is counterproductive to blame parents for their children's problems, it is vital that the parents become involved in the treatment process.

Hearing Impairments

As with most disabling conditions, wide differences exist among students who could be classified along a continuum of hearing impairment. At one end of the scale would be the slightly hard of hearing child whose only special need is to sit or stand within close range of those who are speaking. At the other end might be the congenitally deaf student who has little intelligible speech and who requires considerable educational, social, and personal assistance in order to fulfill his or her potential.

Advances in medical science are rapidly changing the causes and the nature of deafness. In the past, meningitis caused about 10% of all childhood profound hearing loss; today antibiotics are preventing most cases of postlingual deafness and saving the lives of infants who used to die from the disease. Many premature infants are now being saved through medical advances, although these children are often deaf and/or multiply handicapped (Schildroth, 1986).

Characteristics of Deaf Students

Deaf and hard of hearing children are generally representative of the larger society. Intelligence, social class, and educational level of parents are the same as for hearing children. The educational attainment of deaf adults falls one year below that of the general population; however, because of their significantly lower academic achievement, deaf people suffer a significant educational handicap (Moores, 1987).

The older a person is at the time he or she suffered a hearing loss, the less the person is disabled. After a child has acquired speech and the rudiments of abstract concepts, deafness is primarily a hearing handicap. But for the child born deaf, the disability is much greater. The congenitally deaf child is often unable to develop intelligible speech; further, he or she misses the nuances and tones of speech that add significantly to its meaning. The congenitally deaf person necessarily learns that names of objects, activities, and people are exact. Learning is structured to be precise and orderly; eventually, the individual's mental habits and attitudes follow the same literal, exact pattern of operation. It is naturally extremely difficult for the deaf child to learn the meanings of abstract concepts; it follows that the ability to reason in abstract terms is greatly hampered. While there is disagreement regarding the ability of deaf children to use a form of internal verbalization to assist in the process of abstract thinking, deaf children consistently score lower than hearing children on tests and activities requiring abstract reasoning.

Parental Interaction

Ninety percent of deaf children are born to hearing parents, and the vast majority of these parents are unable to communicate manually with their children. The effects of this lack of communication are far-reaching, compromising the child's understanding of the environment, and also serving to prevent the child and his or her parents from truly **knowing** one another and thus developing a strong bond of closeness. Deaf children of deaf parents fare much better. Generally, deaf parents are not as surprised to learn of the deafness of their children and are, therefore, not as traumatized by the event. This fact probably contributes to their ability to more readily cope with the child's handicap. A more important explanation for the closer parent-child relationships when parents are deaf concerns the use of manual communication. Most deaf parents use sign language with their deaf and hearing children. As they communicate, parents can test the child's understanding and they can build closeness based on mutual communication.

Effects of Deafness on Personality Development

The communication barriers that often isolate profoundly deaf people from the larger world of the hearing affect every aspect of a deaf person's life. In general, the more severely impaired a deaf person is, the more restricted that person is in terms of gaining information and experience in the world. Although variations are great, a number of characteristics are associated with people who are profoundly and congenitally deaf.

Often, they are considered to be emotionally immature, egocentric, or lacking empathy for others. Learning to care for others and to respond to others' needs is dependent upon a language of emotions and a system of verbal feedback, areas that are generally unavailable to the deaf child.

Visual Impairments

It is estimated that there are approximately 6.4 million people in the United States who have difficulty seeing, even with corrective lenses. Of these, 1.7 million are severely impaired, which means that they are either legally blind or function as though they are. The concept of blindness has often been misunderstood by people who have interpreted it to mean total absence of light perception. In actuality, few individuals are **totally** blind, although there are many who have so little vision or light perception that they cannot depend on it for mobility or space perception.

As with deafness, congenital blindness appears to be increasing in spite of disease control because advances in acute pediatric care are enabling more children to survive, albeit blind, who would formerly have died.

Cognitive Development

The three major ways in which severe visual impairment limits an individual are in his or her range and variety of experiences, interaction with the environment, and the ability to move about independently. Blind and severely impaired youngsters are necessarily limited experientially in some ways. The child who was blinded before the age of 4 or 5, or example, can have no concept of color, no understanding of perspective, and no comparable knowledge of three-dimensional space. Some concepts are virtually impossible to explain without the benefit of sight because they are too inaccessible (stars), too large (mountains), too small (ants), or too abstract (gravity). However, much of the experiential deprivation that characterizes many blind children could be avoided through the efforts of creative counselors, teachers, and parents. Severely visually impaired children are often observed to be quiet and passive in comparison to their sighted peers, a condition that is usually attributed to inadequate stimulation of the child's other senses. Blind children are frequently overprotected by well-meaning but misguided parents and teachers who suffer every bump and bruise more than do their resilient children.

Interaction with the Environment

Because of limited interaction with the environment, blind children frequently turn inward, and many develop repetitive, self-stimulating behavior such as rocking, eye rubbing, or head bobbing. While such activities are not usually harmful in themselves, they do serve to further separate a blind child from peers. The function of such mannerisms, sometimes called **blindisms,** is not completely known, nor are the causes well understood. The behavior appears to be more frequent when children are either highly stimulated or bored; it seems to be more prevalent among younger children who are more severely impaired and who have relatively low intelligence. However, the behaviors do appear, to varying extent, in the majority of visually impaired children.

Mobility

The restriction in mobility is often considered to be the most serious effect of blindness. Without independent skills in getting from place to place, the blind person is severely hampered in terms of vocational and social independence. Rather than ask for and accept assistance, many blind people forego participation in activities and fall into a pattern of withdrawal. Thus, it is vital that mobility training be started early and that extensive efforts be devoted to its attainment.

Until the student becomes proficient in moving about independently, he or she will need to depend on the services of a sighted guide. It is important that the visually impaired student assume an active role in this process in order to facilitate movement and compensate for unskilled guides. The sighted guide technique is detailed in most general texts concerned with education of blind students. It should be learned by counselors, teachers, and students who will be in contact with severely visually impaired students.

Personal and Social Development

There is no evidence that blindness or visual impairment causes personality problems, and most visually impaired students are remarkably similar to their sighted peers of the same age. However, the environmental forces that interact to cause limitations in the cognitive development of visually impaired youth also have an impact on personal/social development. The self-concept of blind students, for example, is inextricably related to the attitudes and behaviors of others. Blindness has long been shrouded in mystery and fear, and blind people often experience overt avoidance from others, including family and friends. Unless they are unusually aggressive, the cumulative effect is to reduce the amount of social contact, to further the withdrawal and isolation of the blind person, and to inhibit the development of social skills and self-confidence.

Counselors may need to be particularly attuned to the personal/social needs of students with partial sight. Partially sighted students are much less disabled than functionally blind persons because even extremely limited vision allows for the development of concepts in visual terms and aids greatly in mobility and in learning. However, partially sighted students often have more adjustment and social problems than do blind students. The reasons for this situation are not clear, but they may be due to the marginal position that partially sighted children must play. As with other handicapping conditions, counseling, education of others in the school, and success-oriented experiences are primary means by which the visually impaired student, whether blind or partially sighted, can be most successfully integrated into the social environment of the school.

Orthopedic Impairments

Students who are frequently classified as **orthopedically disabled** represent a particularly diverse group since their individual health problems are similar only in the fact that they concern some aspect of the skeletal system. Orthopedic impairments may range from obvious skeletal conditions such as a limb amputation to a disease such as cerebral palsy, which is neurological in origin. Health problems that impair a person's ability to walk and be totally self-sufficient in personal care do result in similar environmental constraints and thus justify grouping for discussion purposes. Counselors and teachers should keep in mind, however, that generalizations based upon a loosely defined category such as orthopedic impairments are not justified and could result in false assumptions and conclusions.

Several different types of orthopedic disabilities that affect school aged children will be described briefly.

Cerebral Palsy

Approximately 550,000 persons in the United States have cerebral palsy, which has been described as "a group of conditions usually originating in childhood, characterized by paralysis, weakness, incoordination or any other aberration of motor function caused by pathology of the motor control centers of the brain. In addition to such motor dysfunction, cerebral palsy may include learning difficulties, psychological problems, sensory defects, convulsions, and behavioral disorders of organic origin (Love & Walthall, 1977, pp. 64–65).

The way in which cerebral palsy is manifested is dependent upon both the cause and the location of cerebral damage. Three types of cerebral palsy are spasticity, dyskinesia, and ataxia. The most prevalent form is the spastic type, encompassing approximately 60% of all cerebral palsy cases. Involvement may be with all four limbs or with one, two, or three. In some types of cerebral palsy, the person may be able to use his or her arms, ambulate and communicate sufficiently; in other types, the person may be completely dependent on attendant care.

Because damaged brain tissue cannot presently be replaced or repaired, there is no cure for cerebral palsy. However, numerous medical treatments and related services have enabled people with cerebral palsy to become increasingly more independent.

Muscular Dystrophy

Muscular dystrophy is the general designation for a group of chronic diseases whose most prominent characteristic is the progressive degeneration of the skeletal or voluntary musculature. There are variations in the age of onset, in the muscle groups first affected, and in the rate of progression. As a rule, it can be said that the earlier the clinical symptoms appear, the more rapid is the progression.

Depending on the type of muscular dystrophy, an individual may be minimally or severely disabled; life expectancy may be significantly shortened or hardly affected. Mental deficiency is not an accompaniment of the condition.

The most common form of muscular dystrophy to affect children is Duchenne's Form, named after the French neurologist who first described it in 1861. Duchenne's muscular dystrophy is primarily a disease of young boys in which muscle tissue degenerates, is replaced by fat, and results in progressive muscle weakness. The rate of progression is slow, although relentless, and is usually fatal by the time a person reaches adulthood. Fortunately, no pain is involved, although children with muscular dystrophy have normal sensation.

Very little formal research has been conducted on the psychosocial aspects of muscular dystrophy. Parental reactions appear to be particularly important in the case of the child with muscular dystrophy. Guilt because the disease is transmitted through a genetic pattern and constant sorrow concerning the slow degeneration and eventual death can easily lead to overprotection, a lack of discipline, and consequently further unnatural psychosocial growth patterns for the child.

Traumatic Spinal Cord Injuries

Spinal cord injuries occur most frequently among those most often involved in physical risk taking: adolescent boys and young men. The degree of impairment depends upon the extent of the damage to the spinal cord and the location of the injury. Injury to the spinal cord in the lower back will result in lack of feeling and movement in the lower extremities, a condition referred to as paraplegia. Damage in the area of the upper back will cause paralysis of the legs and loss of some feeling in the upper torso and arms. Damage to the spinal cord in the neck area will result in loss of sensation and movement in the parts of the body below the injury, often referred to as quadriplegia. At the present time, there are no known means of repairing damage to the spinal cord, so that injury is permanent.

Adjustment to a spinal cord injury is particularly difficult since the disability occurs suddenly, without warning, and generally forces a drastic change in the person's total life-style. In addition to the obvious and traumatic implications of loss of mobility, the spinal cord injured person must cope with other equally drastic body changes. Pressure sores are a serious complication, sometimes requiring corrective surgery. Concerns about sexuality are natural and universal with spinal cord injured people. Bladder and bowel management have social as well as physical ramifications; the degree of self-care possible will, of course, depend upon the extent and point of injury. A person with quadriplegia may be totally dependent upon attendants and mechanical aids, whereas a person who has arm use can assume a great deal of his or her care, may have less difficulty with bladder or bowel management, and can more efficiently prevent pressure sores.

Spina Bifida Myclomeningocele

Spina bifida is, today, the major cause of paraplegia in the young child (Travis, 1976). In addition to paralysis and deformities of the lower body, children with spina bifida frequently have hydrocephalus, are incontinent, and in some cases are mentally retarded.

Spina bifida results from incomplete closure of the lower end of the spinal cord. In severe form (myclomeningocele), the cord bulges out in a sac covered by membrane; in less severe forms, the defect can be repaired surgically; and in some mild forms, the condition may be unknown until discovered accidentally through X-rays.

Children with myclomeningocele are usually incontinent. They may have paralysis of the lower limbs and are prone to fractures. Because of attendant bone and joint deformities, the frequent presence of hydrocephalus, and other physical conditions, most children with spina bifida have undergone numerous surgeries by the time they are of school age.

Adolescence is a particularly difficult time for children with spina bifida. Physical as well as psychological problems increase, and many students slip into periodic despair as they recognize fully their present social limitations and project their future. Because of reduced social contact, the adolescent with myclomeningocele is often not prepared for teenage stress. Parents, counselors, and teachers must insure that the adolescent becomes as independent and socially involved as is realistic, yet recognize and act upon the very real dependency needs in certain areas.

Other Diseases and Health Conditions

A number of diseases or chronic health conditions are prevalent enough among school-aged youth to warrant inclusion in this chapter. Again, there is no functional means of grouping the conditions because of their innate diversity and the variability of their effects. Probably the one thing they do have in common is the fact that, to some degree, they restrict daily activities.

Asthma

Asthma, the most common chronic disease of childhood, affecting more than 1,500,000 children in the United States, is a disorder of respiration with repeated episodes of difficulty in breathing, characterized by wheezing, labored breathing, cough, and sputum. These symptoms may range from the mildest cough and wheeze to respiratory distress of such severity as to obstruct breathing with fatal consequences. The usual cause of asthma derives from an allergic disorder.

Asthma is primarily a disease of early and middle childhood, usually receding during adolescence. It is most frequent among Caucasians and is twice as common among boys as girls. Asthmatic attacks often begin with a short cough, chilling, and a runny nose, to be followed by wheezing as the child gasps for breath. Attacks frequently last several hours in spite of medication; an attack continuing for 24 hours or more is commonly referred to as **status** (status asthmaticus) and should be regarded as an emergency.

The particular substances or conditions that trigger an asthmatic attack are frequently difficult to pinpoint. Some specialists consider emotions to be influential in instigating an asthmatic attack, and during the past few years much research has pointed to a relationship between asthma and parent-child relationships.

The asthmatic child has been described as emotionally sensitive and typically negativistic, lacking self confidence, and having feelings of inferiority. Some of these characterizations must be attributed to the fear-inducing anxiety attacks that the student suffers, to academic difficulties caused by missing numerous days of school, and to the complex familial relationships often brought about as a result of the illness.

Sickle Cell Anemia

Sickle cell anemia is a painful, inherited blood disorder found predominately in black children. The sickle cell **trait** occurs in approximately 10% of American blacks; these individuals do not have the disease itself, although under some circumstances such as anoxia, shock, or respiratory infection complications due to the trait can ensue.

Sickle cell anemia itself appears in about 1 of 400 black people. For some reason, a number of normally round, flexible red blood cells distort themselves into elongated crescents or sickle shapes. The rigidity of the sickle shaped cells prevent their passing through tiny blood vessels; instead they **logjam** the capillaries, causing damage or death to certain tissues. These occasions are called **pain crises.**

Pain crises vary considerably in intensity, duration, and frequency. In some children, episodes may occur every few days; in others, they may be years apart. The child's back, chest, arms, and legs may be painful;

joints may swell; the child may become drowsy, feverish, unable to speak; he or she might develop nosebleeds, bloody urine, or other symptoms (Travis, 1976).

No cure presently exists for sickle cell anemia; treatment is generally confined to minimizing conditions that trigger an episode and to relieving the pain associated with a crisis. Crises are precipitated by infection, chilling, dehydration, strenuous exercise, sweating, changes in barometric pressures, and other situations that increase the body's demand for oxygen. One difficulty associated with prevention is the fact that until recently sickle cell anemia was not recognized among the general population, and it has been subject to much misunderstanding. At this point in time, studies concerning the psychosocial effects of sickle cell anemia are virtually nonexistent.

Epilepsy

Epilepsy is a condition caused by intermittent imbalance of electrical activity of the brain. It is manifested in seizures that may be of several different types. Several of the most common forms of seizure are grand mal, petit mal, and psychomotor seizures. Grand mal is characterized by loss of consciousness, followed progressively by muscle rigidity, flailing of the limbs, and the entire body becoming limp. Upon regaining consciousness, the person may have a headache, feel tired, and be somewhat uncoordinated for a while. During a petit mal seizure, the individual loses consciousness only momentarily; the person stares and eyelids may twitch. Petit mal seizures usually last only a few seconds, whereas a grand mal seizure may continue for several minutes.

Although 80% of seizures can be totally or partially controlled through medication, epilepsy remains a mysterious and frightening condition to many people. The stigma attached to epilepsy is pervasive, demonstrated by the frequent reference to seizures as "fits" in professional literature as well as in lay conversation. While epilepsy itself requires no special treatment other than preventative medication and a balanced regimen in terms of sleep and nutrition, discrimination in employment and social settings is persistent. Adjustment to epilepsy is difficult since seizures are so unpredictable.

Diabetes

Diabetes mellitus is a metabolic disease of unknown origin in which lack of insulin production prevents utilization of carbohydrates for energy;

instead, the food intended for fuel—sugar—bypasses normal routes and spills into the blood and from there into the urine, being lost for strength and energy. (Travis, 1976).

Although lay literature emphasizes the normality of life accessible to youngsters with diabetes, death and disability rates are extremely high. In order to control the disease as much as possible, the relationship between food ingested, insulin injected, and energy expended must be properly balanced. Children, their parents, and school personnel must be watchful for two potential hazards: insulin reaction and diabetic coma. Insulin reaction or hypoglycemia occurs when food intake is too small or exercise too great to maintain the necessary balance. Trembling, sweating, dizziness, or vomiting are warning signals; a full-scale reaction can be prevented by ingesting orange juice, chocolate, or some other quickly burning sugar. Coma occurs when too much sugar is present, as when the child has overindulged in sugar-laden foods, when physical activity is lessened, or when minor ailments such as colds are present.

The psychosocial problems associated with juvenile diabetes are, for the most part, similar to those affiliated with other disabilities. Particularly during adolescence, the child may rebel against treatments, viewing them as conditions that appear to emphasize his or her differences. Additionally, the diabetic child must cope with the problems associated with daily injections, urine tests, and diet regimentation.

COMMON EXPERIENCES OF STUDENTS WITH DISABILITIES

The number of debilitating childhood diseases and other health conditions that serve to alter a student's life-style and that have definite psychosocial implications is long. Outwardly, the various conditions may have little in common. Some may appear to be more serious in that they are generally considered fatal. Others may seem to have more drastic ramifications for the intrafamilial relationship. Some are particularly insidious because of their progressive and degenerative nature. Many of the diseases are relatively rare, such as diabetes, which strikes only 1 in 3000 children. The disease and conditions described, however, do have several common characteristics. First, they have significant psychological ramifications for the individual. Some, such as asthma, appear to be precipitated by stress or other emotional conditions. Others, such as epilepsy, are accompanied by negative reactions of others that are far more debilitating than the condition itself. In all the conditions discussed, the psychosocial implications extend to the family. In some, the necessity for continual and intensive treatment conducted in the home may result in intense mother-child relationships. The possibility of alienation and feelings of rejection by other family members is strong; difficulties in separating from the mother may appear in spite of natural strivings for independence at adolescence. Financial problems may intensify as the child grows older and requires more sophisticated treatment or equipment. Daily and regimented care of the child may preclude a normal, spontaneous life for the entire family, with family outings and vacations virtually unknown (Lombana, 1992).

Children with chronic diseases and health conditions share the various agonies of adolescence with their nondisabled peers. However, for the chronically ill child, the necessity for various treatments, alterations in body structure, and their frequent inability to participate in the normal physical and social activities of teenagers accentuate their differences. Counselors need to be particularly sensitive to the concerns of these students.

From a medical standpoint, each condition varies considerably in its effects upon a person; factors such as age of onset and severity of the condition help determine the medical prognosis. Even more variable than the medical factors are the psychological variables that govern the effects of a given disability on the adjustment and lifestyle of an individual. It appears that a person's characteristic response patterns and personality variables are the most influential elements in the determination of his or her reaction to a handicap. Thus, it becomes impossible to discuss a psychology of disability apart from the psychology of individuals.

Although there appears to be little definitive relationship between personality and a given type of disability, the fact that a disability exists does have ramifications for personality development. Statistics repeatedly show that disabled persons in general are more maladjusted than nondisabled people (Wallender & Hubert, 1987). A closer look reveals a number of factors that alter the environment in which the disabled person develops and responds. Societal reactions to disability are highly aversive and serve to reinforce negative self-images.

Although the reactions of the general public influence the self-perceptions of disabled persons, these influences are minimal in comparison with the effect of the family. The disability of a child clearly pervades and alters the entire family constellation. Parents, in particular, must cope with the burden of the handicap from medical, financial, and psychological perspectives. No matter what the disability, the parents undergo a grief process that is frequently more profound than that experienced by the child. The parents must cope the financial aspects of disability, which in some instances are staggering, both in terms of actual cost and in the constancy of the burden. Parents are very often the primary treatment givers, which results in a complex and intense relationship with the disabled child. Parents must deal not only with the disabled child and his or her problems but also with other familial involvements, including the marital relationship and the needs of siblings.

On a more positive note, research consistently indicates that regardless of the particular condition involved, disabled people are more like than unlike nondisabled persons. Adjustment to disability appears to be successful for most individuals. Most do not differ from their nondisabled classmates in such diverse variables as socioeconomic status of parents, school track, self-concept, and educational and occupational aspirations. In terms of general life satisfaction, disabled people are as **happy** as nondisabled people, in spite of the fact that the disabled persons consider their lives to be more difficult.

Chapter Three

ATTITUDES TOWARD STUDENTS
WITH DISABILITIES

At the age of seven, Harold Krents, a blind student, was in a regular second-grade class. He had no trouble mastering the academic work, but when he tried to join his male classmates in a battle against the girls, he was told in no uncertain terms that he was not a member of their group.

> "What are you doing here?" one rather large recruit asked.
> "I've come to fight with you," I replied.
> "We don't want you," said the entire army of boys.
> I stood there in stunned disbelief. "Why not?" I asked angrily, "I'm a boy."
> "Yes, but you're blind," said the large recruit.
> "Only some," I said defensively.
> "You are blind," he repeated. The way he said it made me flinch.
> "I'm a boy first and blind second," I said quietly.
> "No, you're not, you're a blind boy."
> For some reason, the entire army of boys found this very amusing, and raucous laughter reverberated through the playground (Krents, 1972, p. 63).

Negative attitudes can be more debilitating and damaging to people who are handicapped than the disabilities themselves. School-aged youth, who are involved with the development of a self-identity, who are learning social skills, who are growing academically, and who are planning for a future in the work world are especially susceptible to devaluation by others. Derision and rejection by a student's peers, as illustrated in the anecdote concerning Harold Krents, can have a profoundly negative effect on the self-confidence and self-esteem of an impressionable youngster. Avoidance and lowered expectations of teachers, counselors, and other adults in the educational environment can greatly hamper a student's motivation to achieve academically and to actively participate in society. On the other hand, positive and accepting attitudes and behaviors can go far toward helping a handicapped student achieve self-respect and self-confidence, develop good interpersonal skills, and move toward taking an independent and productive role in the world of work.

Attitudes are complex and far-reaching; as such, they hold implications for every aspect of guidance for students with disabilities. Because of the profound influence of attitudes, counselors need to assume one role that is not traditionally considered a specific guidance function: developing and implementing programs to foster positive attitudes toward students with handicaps. This role may become the single most important aspect of a counselor's work with students with disabilities. In order to be able to fulfill this responsibility, counselors need to have a broad understanding of the nature of attitudes, knowledge of the beliefs and stereotypes that constitute attitudes toward people with disabilities, empathy for the effects of negative attitudes on students with handicaps, and skill with specific methods of fostering positive attitudes.

THE COMPOSITION OF ATTITUDES

Attitudes may be thought of as positive or negative emotional reactions to an object, reactions that are accompanied by specific beliefs and that tend to impel the individual to behave in certain ways toward the object of the attitude. More simply stated, an attitude is a tendency to respond in either a positive or a negative way to something or someone. All people hold many attitudes toward a wide variety of topics. People may have attitudes toward mystery novels, chocolate ice cream, capital punishment, beards, or people with handicaps. People may hold attitudes toward marriage, divorce, pollution, blindness, deafness, or mainstreaming. Attitudes vary in strength, depending upon factors such as early learning experiences, availability of factual information, influences of significant others, and the extent to which an attitude is part of a larger system of beliefs. These and other factors influence the intensity of feelings and help determine the ease or difficulty with which a given attitude can be changed.

Because they represent tendencies to respond in a given way, people can and often do observe or infer an attitude through behavior. For example, if a student consistently makes good grades in school, people might assume that the student has a **positive attitude** toward school. However, attitudes cannot always be inferred from behavior. For example, the high achieving student may produce out of a need for attention, fear of parental reprisal, or fear of failure rather than from a genuine desire to learn and a positive attitude toward school.

GENERAL ATTITUDES TOWARD PEOPLE WITH DISABILITIES

It has been difficult to determine how the general public feels about persons with handicaps. It appears that when asked direct questions, the majority of the general public indicate that they hold positive attitudes toward people with disabilities. Several studies have shown that people with handicaps are held in higher esteem than are the nonhandicapped. Yet, when behavior toward people with disabilities is examined or when subjects are asked to characterize handicapped persons, the results are essentially negative. Very often, people with disabilities are avoided, pitied, or patronized. They are viewed as less intelligent, less happy, less enjoyable to be with, and less likable than nondisabled people. In one study (Makas, 1988), disabled and nondisabled people were found to have very different ideas of what constitutes a "positive attitude" toward persons with handicaps. For the disabled respondents, positive attitudes concerned being viewed and treated the same as other people, whereas the nondisabled respondents thought positive attitudes were reflected in desires to be nice, helpful, and ultimately placing people with disabilities in a needy position. Even when positive attitudes are expressed, they are often based on myths and false assumptions, such as the idea that blind people are endowed with superior hearing or that physically handicapped persons are blessed with virtue as a reward for suffering (Patterson & Witten, 1987).

Whatever the direction of stereotypic views, positive or negative, people with disabilities are seen as essentially **different** from nonhandicapped people, an attitude that in itself contributes to the isolation of people with disabilities. The perception of the **difference** of people with disabilities appears to pervade the thinking of most individuals, regardless of demographic or geographic characteristics.

Peer and Educator Attitudes

Outside their immediate family, the most significant influences on the growth and development of children occur in the school environment. For many students with handicaps, entrance into mainstreamed classes represents their first prolonged contact with nonhandicapped peers. Some disabled youngsters attend integrated schools from the age of 3, while others may have spent several years in residential schools or special classes before being mainstreamed. When a handicapped child enters a regular class, other children might be expected to respond initially with apprehension to the unfamiliar situation.

Unfortunately, research has shown that negative attitudes do not automatically disappear over time. Attitudes of children toward their handicapped peers appear to form and manifest themselves in specific behaviors very early. Gerber (1977) discovered that 4-year-old children were aware of the physical differences of their handicapped classmates, a finding that was confirmed by Weinberg (1978). She noticed that only 17% of the 3-year-old children in her sample were able to discern a physical disability, whereas 71% of the 4-year-olds could do so. Further, the older children showed greater bias against playing with handicapped classmates than did the younger children.

Most research indicates that school-aged children hold negative opinions of their disabled classmates. Students who attended self-contained classes for disabled children were viewed less favorably than those who were in resource classes (Bak, Cooper, Dobroth, & Siperstein, 1987). In another study (Stone & LaGreca, 1990) learning disabled students were more neglected and rejected by their classmates than other students.

Little research has investigated the causes of children's rejection of handicapped peers other than a general perception of difference. Because children are generally concerned with physical skills and activities, it may be that students with disabilities are seen as incapable in these areas. In some studies, physical attractiveness appears to be a contributing factor (Bickett & Milich, 1990; Matter & Matter, 1989). In some cases, students who wear hearing aids (Silverman & Klees, 1989) or who have a minor speech impediment (Freeby & Madison, 1989) are viewed by their classmates as less able to perform, academically, socially, or athletically.

Attitudes of educators toward students with disabilities have been studied more frequently than peer attitudes and have resulted in a few general conclusions. Attitudes of classroom teachers have received the most attention, while very few studies have involved school counselors.

Since counselors necessarily work closely with classroom teachers regarding the mainstreaming of children with disabilities, it is important to understand how teachers generally view and respond to these students.

The attitudes of teachers have significant impact on the intellectual, social, and emotional development of students. Teacher attitudes affect behavior in a variety of ways. For example, positive attitudes are related to the amount, degree, and quality of interaction that occurs between a teacher and his or her student. A teacher who is comfortable with a student is more likely to talk to the student, to maintain eye contact, and to give positive reinforcement. Likewise, if the teacher holds negative attitudes toward a student, that teacher is more likely to avoid interaction, to reduce eye contact, and to give negative reinforcement. Alves and Gottlieb (1986) found that teachers in 38 elementary classrooms asked fewer questions and gave less feedback to learning disabled students than to others. In another study (Kistner & Gatlin, 1989), teachers responded negatively to students who were unpopular or withdrawn.

The expectations that teachers have for their students' classroom performance develop from attitudes and have implications for the achievement of the students and the ways in which the students come to view themselves. The effect of teacher expectations was vividly portrayed in the well-known Pygmalian study (Rosenthal & Jacobson, 1968). In that study, elementary school teachers were falsely told that certain children were **late bloomers** and could be expected to make substantial gains in their academic achievement during the school year. Although there were no significant differences between the experimental and control groups at the beginning of the year, the experimental group showed marked gains over the control group in IQ and academic progress during the course of the study. The differences were attributed to teacher expectations.

Research specifically concerned with teacher attitudes toward students with disabilities has produced somewhat ambiguous results. One reason for the inconclusiveness of findings is that research methodology and instrumentation have varied widely, preventing direct comparisons. Some conclusions, however, can be drawn from research conducted in recent years.

Sex, age, race, and teaching experience have relatively little impact on teacher attitudes. While a few studies have found that younger teachers and those with less than seven years teaching experience have more favorable attitudes toward students with disabilities, most research indicates that attitudes cannot be predicted on these variables (Rogers, 1987).

Teachers with greater knowledge of handicapping conditions have more positive attitudes than do teachers with lesser knowledge. Lack of experience with disabled students is a primary contributor to the fears and prejudices of many educators. In one study (Lass, Tecca, & Woodford, 1987) a group of 113 classroom teachers was surveyed regarding their attitudes toward students who wear hearing aids. The authors report that many of the teachers felt uncomfortable talking to people with hearing aids and believed that hearing aid wearers were embarrassed about the devices. Conversely, special education teaching experience, number of courses taken in special education, and special education in-service experience are related to positive attitudes (Fabre & Walker, 1987).

The Development of Attitudes

Precisely how attitudes are formed and developed remains a mystery, although it is known that attitudes are learned. Several theories regarding particular aspects of behavior can contribute to understanding of the development of attitudes toward people with disabilities. In studies of reactions of both people and animals to distorted bodies, Hebb (1946) concluded that a conflict in perception occurs when an object is perceived as both similar and dissimilar to its usual state. This conflict, which is analogous to the perception generated toward people with distorted, disfigured, or **different** physical characteristics, manifests itself in fear and avoidance.

A theory more concerned with human relationships was developed by Heider (1958). According to Heider, there is an interdependence between a person's liking for another and the feeling of similarity to that person. Also there is a tendency for dissimilar or different people or situations to evoke negative reactions. Unfamiliar people or circumstances, then, result in a sense of threat and an urge to withdraw.

Although the relationships between similarity and attraction (and, conversely, dissimilarity and rejection) are not clear-cut, some parallels can be seen in terms of responses to people with handicaps. As long as people are responded to solely or primarily in terms of their **different** characteristics, a certain emotional distance, if not antipathy, can be expected to occur.

The environmental roots of prejudice toward people with disabilities can be attributed to several factors: social customs and norms, child rearing practices, maintenance of irrational childhood fears, and discrimination-provoking behavior by people with disabilities themselves (Gellman, 1959). These factors interact to build and maintain negative attitudes and behaviors.

Western social customs regarding handicaps have evolved from a variety of historical views: "the Greek belief that the physically impaired were inferior; the pre-prophetic Hebraic idea that the sick were being punished by God; the early Christian faith that the handicapped acquire moral virtue because of their illness; and the Darwinian theory of the survival of the fittest" (Gellman, 1959, p.4). This conglomeration of inherited views has resulted in marked ambivalence toward people with disabilities. Society overtly stresses the importance of health and wholeness and subtly encourages its members to be accountable for the state of their physical or mental well-being.

Parents expect, and are expected, to produce **perfect** replicas of themselves. The most important consideration for an expectant parent is that the offspring be **normal.** Profound relief is the instantaneous response to a normal child, and intense guilt is often evoked by the birth of a handicapped baby. Many parents continue to live in constant anxiety that their child will become disabled, and this anxiety carries over into the irrational reluctance of parents to allow their children to interact socially with people with disabilities.

Ultimately, children reflect their parents' fears regarding disability, as well as their emphasis on conformity in appearance and behavior. As adolescents and adults, they react in various ways. Peer pressure causes many young people to disparage handicapped individuals.

People with disabilities have undoubtedly contributed to their own devaluation. In their efforts to find others with whom to identify, handicapped adolescents frequently seek the companionship of other people with disabilities. Within such subgroups, people tend to become acclimated to a learned helplessness position (Campbell, Cull & Hardy, 1986).

Behavioral Reactions to People with Disabilities

Research has shown that a major response toward handicapped individuals is avoidance. Avoidance behaviors vary along a continuum from overt rejection to discomfort in social situations and limitations in eye contact. The degree of avoidance behavior exhibited depends upon a variety of factors, including the nature and extent of the disability, the self-concept of the nonhandicapped individual, and prior exposure to the disabling condition. Less clearly understood are the cognitive and affective processes a person experiences that interact to produce the avoidance behavior.

Psychotherapist Albert Ellis (1962) derived a counseling approach based on his theory of dysfunctional behavior. Essentially, the theory postulates three stages: A, the **activating** event; B, a person's **belief** or thoughts regarding the event; and C, the **consequences** or feelings generated as a result of the beliefs. According to Ellis and other rational or cognitive theorists, an event or stimulus does not result directly in feelings or physiological responses. Instead, a cognitive process occurs at point B that links the two. This cognitive process involves a conscious or unconscious statement about the event, which leads to the feeling response at point C. To illustrate the process in terms of reactions to people with disabilities, an activating event, A, might be an unexpected confrontation with a disfigured person. C, the physiological consequence, could be represented by discomfort or anxiety. But C is not caused by A. Instead, an intervening variable, B, occurs, which could be a self statement such as, "That person has something I might catch," or "That person is so different from me that we have nothing in common." A behavioral reaction, such as avoidance, generally follows the emotional response.

Following the cognitive theory, it appears that when first confronted with a visibly handicapped individual, many people tell themselves a host of irrational statements that lead to emotional and behavioral reactions. Some of the more common statements, consciously or unconsciously expressed, include the following:

- If he is blind (or deaf, or whatever), he must be totally incapacitated.
- Her disability may be contagious.
- Because she is orthopedically impaired (or learning disabled, or whatever) we have absolutely nothing in common.
- He must be constantly miserable and unhappy because of his handicap.

Observing the behavior of nondisabled people toward handicapped individuals offers a truer picture of their real feelings that do verbal reports. The fact that many people report favorable attitudes yet respond physiologically quite differently indicates both the power of social trends and the strength of internal beliefs.

CHANGING ATTITUDES TOWARD
STUDENTS WITH DISABILITIES

Since attitudes are learned, they can be changed or unlearned. The **unlearning** process may be simple or complex, depending on the strength and nature of the attitudes held. It is generally easier to develop positive attitudes in a person whose present feelings are neutral than it is to reverse extremely negative attitudes. It is usually easier to develop positive attitudes in children than in adults, since the views of children are seldom firmly entrenched. But whether the counselor's focus is on students or teachers, on fostering positive feelings or overcoming negative stereotypes, it is essential that the process be implemented through sound, empirically tested approaches rather than depending upon haphazard, trial and error methods.

Three general means of changing negative attitudes toward handicaps and people with disabilities have been tested through research: contact, information, and simulation. They have met with varying degrees of success.

Contact

Contact with handicapped persons has been frequently cited as a vital element in reversing negative stereotypes. The idea is that as handicapped and nonhandicapped people interact, the **differences** of the two groups will dissipate and anxiety will lessen. But, the nature of the contact must be carefully considered. While a few researchers have found that mere physical integration of children with disabilities into regular school programs increased positive attitudes toward them, other attempts have been less successful (Thomas, Foreman, & Remenyi, 1985). Structured contact, such as through peer tutoring (Brown, 1986; Fenrick & Petersen, 1984), classroom projects, and small group activities (Stevens & Allen, 1984) have been more successful in lowering barriers and creating friendships among children. In one study (Haring, Breen, Pitts-Conway, & Lee, 1987) fifteen tutors and fifteen special friends drawn from a high school population interacted daily with a class of nine autistic students of varying ages. Both the tutors and special friends showed significant gains on an attitudinal scale, and the quality of interaction between the helpers and their charges improved markedly by the end of the project.

In another study (Newberry & Parrish, 1987) a large group of girl scouts and boy scouts dramatically increased their social contacts with disabled students after prolonged and structured interaction.

Many educators seem to make a naive assumption that merely integrating students with disabilities into regular school programs will serve to foster understanding and acceptance. Research evidence contradicts such a conclusion. Contact appears to be most effective when it is designed to produce prolonged or very personal interaction.

Information

Although some studies have found that individuals with extensive knowledge about handicapping conditions also hold positive attitudes toward handicapped persons, there is little evidence that cognitive knowledge alone will produce attitude change. Structured educational programs specifically designed to increase knowledge and understanding have resulted in positive attitude change in both teachers and students (Mathews, White, & Mrdjenovich-Hanks, 1990). However, most other research has not been successful. In one study (Sanders & Sanders, 1987) a group of undergraduate students in Education were exposed to a series of lectures and video presentations to provide them with accurate information regarding handicapping conditions. In spite of the increased knowledge, the attitudes of the teachers-to-be did not improve.

Contact and Information

While contact alone and information alone have produced, at best, equivocal results, a combination of approaches has been more successful in changing negative attitudes. Information presented through children's literature (Salend & Moe, 1983) or through professional presentations (Leyser & Price, 1985) coupled with structured contact has been shown to be an effective means of improving children's attitudes toward their handicapped peers.

Simulation, Information, and Contact

In recent years, some efforts to foster positive attitudes toward people with disabilities have employed techniques that involve activities such as role playing and role reversal, as well as other exercises designed to help an individual experience—albeit to a limited degree—the world of a handicapped person. Although most programs employing simulation and other affective techniques have not been tested empirically, the few that have been reported have produced positive changes.

In one study (Lombana, Pratt, and Clawson, 1983) fourth grade children participated in a program that consisted of blindfolded exercises, discussions of stories about blind people, films, and a classroom visit by two blind children from a residential school. The children's attitudes at the conclusion of the program were significantly more positive than those of a control group. More recently, Fiedler and Simpson (1987) developed two different curriculums to improve attitudes toward students with disabilities. Both treatments took place over a ten-week period and included opportunities for contact, information, and simulation activities. Both resulted in improved attitudes, although the more successful approach focused on specific handicaps rather than on the general concept of disability. In a comparative study (Florian & Kehat, 1987), the researchers found that attitudes of high school students toward their disabled peers were significantly improved when they were presented with a variety of activities and approaches, including contact, information, and role-playing.

In summary, the literature concerned with developing positive attitudes toward people with disabilities suggests that change is more likely when the life experiences of people with disabilities can be momentarily touched upon by those who are not handicapped. Simulation activities are a way of developing empathy and learning that, in spite of a handicap, people with disabilities are more like than unlike their nonhandicapped peers. When these approaches are combined with accurate information, the chances of reversing negative attitudes or developing positive ones are enhanced.

THE COUNSELOR'S ROLE IN ATTITUDE CHANGE

Attitudes toward students with disabilities profoundly influence the ability of those students to succeed within the mainstream of their educational environment. Therefore, all activities that counselors conduct on behalf of their disabled students—individual and group counseling, consultation with teachers, career planning, working with parents, and many other guidance functions—are predicated on the development of healthy and nonprejudicial attitudes. However, it is not enough for counselors to be aware of others' attitudes or to help students with disabilities cope with those feelings and behaviors that can threaten to destroy self-esteem. A primary role of the counselor with regard to students with disabilities is to foster positive attitudes by direct intervention with the students and educational staff within the school. If the counselor were successful in accomplishing this goal, students with disabilities would become mainstreamed in the most positive sense of the word. Teachers with positive attitudes would welcome students with handicaps into their classes, understanding that each is a unique individual who shares many common characteristics with other students of a given age. Differential performance expectations based on labels would not exist because the perceptions of **difference** would disappear as attitudes improve. The other students in the school would neither avoid nor patronize their handicapped peers. As with teachers, as the concept of **difference** would fade, so would the fear, apprehension, and discomfort associated with confronting the unknown. The self-confidence and self-esteem of students with disabilities themselves would soar; being viewed and treated by their peers and teachers as individuals rather than as **handicapped** individuals would enable them to view themselves in the same light. They would feel free to participate in all aspects of their education as **insiders** rather than as **outsiders.** With healthy self-esteem, they would be able to fulfill their individual academic promises, to develop appropriate social and interpersonal skills, and to look forward to a future based on their own strengths and interests rather than one predetermined by others' expectations of their limitations.

Although developing positive attitudes will not always be an easy task for the counselor, it is one that is guaranteed to be productive and rewarding. The opportunity to watch students and teachers discard old fears and develop welcoming attitudes is a reward unto itself. The activities and interchanges involved in attitudinal programs are invariably exciting and appealing to helping professionals. The opportunities for creative programing are limitless. Fortunately, activities and exercises to change attitudes can be accomplished with little financial resources or specialized training, so that the primary requisites of the counselor are commitment and energy.

Activities to Develop Positive Attitudes

Only the counselor's imagination restricts the great variety of activities that can be used to improve attitudes toward students with disabilities.

Drawings, questionnaires, checklists, and values activities can all be used to help students and teachers recognize and discuss their attitudes toward people with disabilities. Often, people will verbalize positive or socially acceptable attitudes that they do not really feel. Also, some people, particularly young children, may not be consciously aware of their attitudes. As in all discussions of an affective nature, the counselor must refrain from evaluative statements and concentrate on helping participants to clarify their own attitudes. Instead of moralizing or probing, the counselor should accept feelings of pity or apprehension that are expressed. Positive outcomes can be generated through comments designed to promote self-examination, tolerance of differing views, and openness to new information.

Books and films can be used to impart information and help students and teachers become sensitized to the problems and strengths of people with disabilities. Bibliotherapy (see Chapter 4 for a more detailed discussion) can help people identify with others, reduce apprehension, and answer questions that students might be reluctant to discuss in class. The reading of a book or viewing of a film should always be followed by class discussion that focuses on the feelings of the characters involved and the participants' reactions to those feelings.

Activities that help participants simulate particular handicaps provide enormous insight into the daily lives of people with disabilities. To simulate problems of fine motor coordination, participants can tie shoes, button coats, play jacks, or pick up coins while wearing heavy gloves. To illustrate some of the problems that blind people must cope with, blindfolded teachers and/or students can try drinking from a water fountain, counting change, eating, and getting from place to place in the school building. Perceptual disorders can be simulated by requiring participants to reconstruct a design on a card while viewing its visual image in a mirror. The world of deaf people can be illustrated by showing a short movie without sound and asking participants questions about it.

Classroom visits by people who are disabled or who are closely associated with people with disabilities are effective means of providing credible information. Students with disabilities, particularly if they are of the same age as the regular students, provide opportunities for the development of empathy and identification. Disabled adults who are successful in various careers can help dispel myths regarding the dependence and nonproductivity of people with disabilities. Parents of children with disabilities, too, are excellent sources of information, particularly for groups of teachers who will be receiving students with handicaps into their classrooms. The struggles and triumphs of parents are often moving accounts that help develop empathy and understanding; at the same time, parents can provide valuable information regarding learning styles and social maturity of children with various disabilities. Other important sources of information are professionals who work directly with students with disabilities, such as physical, occupational, or speech therapists, mobility instructors, or special education teachers. They can help both students and teachers gain a better understanding of the skills that can be developed through therapy, mobility training, and other procedures, as well as the types of modifications that may be needed in teaching or classroom arrangement.

Role playing is a dynamic and extremely effective method of changing attitudes because it encompasses a variety of affective and cognitive experiences. It is effective with children of all ages as well as with adults. Role playing can be accomplished by having two or three individuals serve as actors while the remainder of the group observes, or the entire group can have specific roles to enact. It can vary from unstructured to highly structured situations. Participants can role play scenes that frequently present problems for people with handicaps (ordering in a restaurant, purchasing something in a store, being isolated in social settings) or act out scenes from a book or film. With older students and adults, the role of an **alter ego** can add another dimension to the role-playing scene. An **alter ego** stands behind each character; after the character speaks, the alter ego says what he or she perceives the character to be feeling or thinking. The frequent discrepancy between the spoken words and the thoughts of a character illustrate the intricacies of communication and help participants become more aware of their attitudes and the interrelationship between attitudes and behavior.

Examining and using aids for people with handicaps such as wheel chairs, prostheses, hearing aids, or braces will help students satisfy their natural curiosity, reduce fear and anxiety concerning unfamiliar items, and encourage students to view them as part of the natural environment. Local agencies, organizations, and hospitals are generally willing to provide equipment on loan. Because many aids can appear formidable out of context, it is better to demonstrate them in conjunction with a related story or film. Likewise, aids can be better understood and appreciated if they are shown during a class visit by a disabled person or therapist. The ease with which the aids are discussed, as well as their obvious importance to the lives of some people with disabilities, will help remove mystery and show them in a positive light.

Using Materials and Activities Effectively

In addition to careful planning and preparation of program activities, the counselor should be aware of ways in which information, contact, and simulation can be used most effectively. The methods used to impart information, interest level of materials, and appropriate selection of simulation activities can help determine whether or not a program is well received by the participants.

When using books, films, presentations, or other means to provide information concerning handicaps, the counselor should be sure that the message presents both the positive and negative aspects of the situation. Thus, by insisting that people with handicaps have **no** problems to contend with or that they are in **all** respects like nonhandicapped people, the credibility of the message is destroyed. Instead, the focus should be on the similarities **and** the differences, on problems **and** how they are solved.

The source of information is an important determinant of its effectiveness. Presentations by people who are perceived as knowledgeable, trustworthy, prestigious, similar, or familiar are more effective than those given by people without those characteristics. People making speeches or presentations often begin with humorous anecdotes or personal experiences to develop rapport and a sense of trust with the audience. Their backgrounds and accomplishments are frequently mentioned in an effort to have them perceived as knowledgeable. People of similar age, interests, or occupations are often viewed as more credible than those who are vastly different in these respects.

In developing simulation activities, the focus must remain on maximum involvement of the participants. The students or teachers should have opportunities to examine their own beliefs, to participate in role reversals, and to make public commitment to an attitude change. The opportunity to express feelings without negative evaluation is a point that cannot be overemphasized. The counselor's primary responsibility in simulation activities is to facilitate participants' self-exploration, analysis, and insight, so that resulting attitude change develops from within and is incorporated into the person's system of values.

Counselor Attitudes toward People with Disabilities

Surprisingly little is known about the attitudes of counselors toward people with handicaps. Some research has indicated that students in counseling have more favorable attitudes toward people with handicaps, but other studies have found no differences in attitudes of counseling students and those majoring in other disciplines.

Until research is generated that probes the beliefs, attitudes regarding mainstreaming, and behavioral intentions of school counselors, it must be assumed that their attitudes do not differ from those of other professionals or from the general population. Thus, counselors may verbalize slightly positive attitudes yet behave in ways that would indicate the opposite. The question then follows: can counselors successfully conduct programs designed to improve attitudes toward students with disabilities if their own views are basically negative? The answer is not as simple as it might appear at face value. It is well known that teaching something to someone else results in additional learning for the instructor. It might be hypothesized, then, that the very process of designing and implementing a program to develop positive attitudes toward handicapped youth would result in more positive attitudes held by the leader. On the other hand, the negative attitudes of the counselor might well reveal themselves during the course of the program, resulting in a damaging experience for all concerned.

How does a counselor go about developing positive attitudes toward people with handicaps? Ideally, he or she should participate in programs or activities such as those suggested in this chapter, activities that focus on a combination of information, contact, and experiential learning. Learning as much as possible about the etiology, as well as the psychology, of various handicaps is a good beginning point. Participation in a graduate class project, professional workshop, or in-service training program is the most effective means of simulating handicapping conditions because it would provide opportunities for interaction and discussion of feelings with others. The committed and motivated counselor, however, could design and implement activities to be accomplished alone or with other members of the guidance staff. However it can be accomplished, the counselor must be comfortable with his or her own attitudes before serving as a model and leader to others.

Chapter Four

COUNSELING STUDENTS WITH DISABILITIES

L ike all people, students with handicaps have basic needs for security, affection, belonging, and achievement. In general, students with disabilities are much more like their nonhandicapped students age-level peers than they are like older or younger people who share only the same disability. Like their peers, children with handicaps need the warmth and security of their parents. As adolescents they seek group identification and peer acceptance; as they move toward young adulthood they become increasingly concerned with their sexual identity. As they continue to mature, they seek increased independence in work and in their social lives. Because handicapped youth share the same basic needs, interests, values, and aspirations as their nondisabled peers, counseling goals and methodologies are also parallel.

Important differences do exist, however, between handicapped and nonhandicapped youth. These differences, which are themselves responsible for the variations required in counseling strategies, are complex and not easily differentiated. A generalization of the counseling needs of students with disabilities, however, might be classified as follows:

- Needs common to all people.
- Needs common to all people within a given age span or developmental stage.
- Needs common to people with handicaps.
- Needs common to handicapped people with similar history (i.e., age at onset or severity of disability).
- Needs common to people with a similar handicapping condition and a similar history.

The list, of course, could continue to be delineated. Characteristics or circumstances such as personality attributes, general health, ethnic origin, socioeconomic status, family constellation, social and educational experiences, or presence of multiple handicap would provide a clearer picture of the myriad counseling needs of people with handicaps. However, even if it were possible to delineate those needs within the confines of this chapter, the description would probably be of limited value to the counselor.

The focus of this chapter will be limited to a brief discussion of the general needs of students with disabilities, basic counseling strategies, a presentation of considerations in counseling students with certain disabilities, and a discussion of some alternative counseling techniques that have proven successful with handicapped students.

The omission of topics such as counselor characteristics, theories of counseling, and the approaches of particular schools of counseling is purposeful. These topics are discussed in numerous texts and are generally available to the counselor through experiential and didactic training in both pre-service and in-service education.

THE COUNSELING NEEDS OF
STUDENTS WITH DISABILITIES

Most handicapped youth who are mainstreamed into regular classrooms or otherwise educated in public school settings have successfully adapted to their disability and will require counseling only for the normal developmental concerns of childhood and adolescence. However, some students may be traumatized by the effects of the disability on their body image or general self-concept, as well as the reactions of others. Most people with disabilities proceed through a dynamic, fluctuating, and often protracted process of adjustment; during this period, counseling may be of vital importance (Livneh & Sherwood, 1991).

Even though many congenitally disabled persons do not experience a traumatic adjustment period, acceptance of their disability is, nevertheless, linked to the reactions of their family members, their peers, and society at large. For psychological health, people with handicaps must come to terms with their disability in the sense of viewing it as a part—but only a part—of them. Danger lies in allowing the handicap to overtake their entire concept of self so that they succumb to the **spread phenomenon.** When this happens, the person with a handicap views himself or herself as totally disabled and helpless and often develops unnecessary psychological dependence on others. The individual can become apathetic and depressed, losing motivation to seek independence and productivity.

At the other end of the continuum are those individuals who strive above all else to be **just like everyone else.** By continuing to deny an aspect of themselves that is, in fact, **different,** they are often unable or unwilling to develop coping strategies that would help make their lives easier. More often than not, continued efforts to deny the disability result in frustration and anger.

With either reaction, the handicapped student is likely to experience difficulties with body image, self-concept, and value structure. The process of re-evaluating one's sense of self—physical, emotional, and spiritual—is a lonely one. A supportive counselor can facilitate this process.

The counseling concerns of students with disabilities, then, may depend greatly on the approach they have taken to adjust to their disability, as well as on their relative success with the adjustment process. Handicapped adolescents and teenagers are likely to be struggling with concerns such as the following:

- How do I retain psychological independence while acknowledging a necessary degree of physical dependence on others?
- How can I cope with my desire to be an average person while acknowledging that in some respects I am not like most people?
- How will I define my sex roles within a society that places value or expectations in areas in which I cannot compete?
- Should I attempt to join the world of the blind (or deaf, or whatever) or make my way in the world of the sighted? What are the implications of my choices?

COUNSELING STUDENTS WITH SPECIFIC HANDICAPS

The specific disabilities of some students can provide the counselor with direction in terms of counseling strategies or approaches. All students experience certain developmental difficulties and, for the most part, counseling methodologies need not vary from one population to another. However, there are considerations and characteristics that are important to the counseling of specific groups.

Counseling Students with Learning Disabilities

The effects of others' perceptions and overt responses on an individual's self-concept are perhaps most vividly and markedly pronounced in the case of students with learning disabilities. The invisibility of the handicap, the frequent occurrences of delayed diagnosis, and the mislabeling of a learning disability as emotional disturbance or mental retardation have all compounded the difficulties that confront these students. Parents become frustrated and exhausted trying to cope with a child who is constantly in motion, who appears to have little control over his or her emotions, or whose behavior is sometimes dangerously impulsive. Classroom teachers may become discouraged trying to teach a child who, while obviously bright, continues to reverse letters and words, who fails to follow moderately simple directions, or who is constantly distracted by extraneous noises. Peers of all ages can be overtly rejecting of students who are clumsy and awkward in sports activities, who appear to be constant bullies, or who erupt into temper tantrums when games don't go their way. Children with learning disabilities usually have little understanding of their own handicap, and they may have no awareness of the effect of their behaviors on others. What the children do see is that in spite of all of their efforts, they simply do not measure up to others' expectations. Repeated instances of being referred to as lazy, selfish, wild, incorrigible, or dumb inevitably lead to feelings of discouragement, worthlessness, and defeat. If not checked, the cycle of self-fulfilling expectations may lead to overt and dangerous acting-out behavior.

The debilitating side effects of learning disabilities have been demonstrated in numerous studies. In comparison with nonhandicapped students, learning disabled students have the following characteristics:

- They have less personal and social competence (Toro, Weissberg, Guare, & Liebenstein, 1990)
- They have more dependent personalities (Margalit, 1984)
- They have higher delinquency rates (Fleener, 1987)
- They have lower self concepts (Wright & Stimmel, 1984)
- They are more involved with drugs (Wright & Stimmel, 1984)
- Their leisure activities are more passive and accompanied by more feelings of loneliness (Margalit, 1984)
- They have more conflictual relationships with their families (Toro, et al., 1990)
- They have more suicidal thoughts (Wright & Stimmel, 1984)

In order to counter the devastating effects of academic and social failure on the self-concept and expectations for future success, learning disabled children must receive three basic forms of assistance. They need help in coping with specific learning and behavioral problems; they need environmental constraints to facilitate the development of particular skills; and they need a great deal of support, reassurance, and positive reinforcement to help build self-esteem and confidence. The needs of students with learning disabilities point to the necessity for counselors to reach beyond traditional counseling methods. Individual and group counseling that focuses on relationship building and self-exploration is valuable. In addition, the counselor should use a variety of structured activities, establish opportunities for the student to attain success, and involve parents and teachers in the overall counseling and rehabilitative program.

Helping a student become involved in activities in which he or she can excel and gain prestige may not reflect traditional notions of counseling, but such methods may have greater benefits than verbal explorations of the student's problems. Participating in art, music, or crafts; operating audiovisual equipment; acting as a library assistant; or tutoring younger children are examples of activities that not only have intrinsic learning value but also serve to enhance self-esteem.

Environmental manipulation is increasingly recognized as a legitimate counseling function and, in many instances, may be the most effective means of helping children. In the case of students with learning disabilities, environmental regulation focuses on the three R's of routine, regularity, and repetition as means of minimizing distractions, developing concentration, and helping to develop inner controls. Both at school and at home, the child needs firmness, planned activities at regular times, simplicity in directions and tasks, concrete materials, and an abundance of positive reinforcement. While the counselor can implement facilitative conditions by eliminating distractions and establishing routine procedures in the counseling situation, he or she can further help by working with parents and teachers to extend the controls into the child's larger environment.

Counseling Students with Mental Handicaps

The dearth of literature concerning therapy with mentally handicapped people is partially the result of a number of erroneous but widespread myths. It has been assumed that the social-emotional needs of people with mental handicaps are essentially different from those of others. Retarded individuals have been viewed as not needing counseling because of a false assumption that they experience less emotional pain than do other people. Many people have assumed that because of their deficits in verbal skills, mentally handicapped individuals would be unable to benefit from counseling.

The facts are, of course, that people with mental handicaps experience the same range of emotional experience and needs as other people. Because of their lower level of intellectual functioning and frequent rejection by others, they often experience more frustration in meeting their own needs. Subsequent low self-esteem, acting out, apathy, and withdrawal present a definite need for counseling that has not been met. Many students with mental handicaps are further hampered by academic failure, particularly since they must live in a society that values educational achievement. Lack of maturity and inappropriate social behaviors lead to rejection and difficulties in employment. Students with mental handicaps are viewed more negatively than virtually all other disability groups, and they frequently experience overt rejection. Thus, the need for counseling in the school setting may be great, particularly at two junctures. When mentally handicapped children first enter school, they need help understanding and accepting their limitations while building on their strengths. Second, during adolescence, the students require support and techniques to enable them to achieve independence, develop appropriate social behaviors, and make emotional adjustments that are typical of their age.

As with all students, the relationship that is established between the counselor and the mentally handicapped child is a crucial determinant of the success of counseling efforts. Some practical suggestions for counselors working with these students include the following:

- The counselor should have a broad understanding of the characteristics associated with the disability and should become knowledgeable of a given student's level of cognitive functioning.
- The counselor needs to possess a sense of humor and be able to cope with personal or irrelevant questions or comments.
- The counselor should use frequent repetition and clarification to insure understanding. The use of tangible aids can help overcome problems in dealing with abstract concepts.
- The counselor should speak in concrete terms and with simple words and sentences. A comment such as, "The way you treat others will often determine how they treat you" may be too complex for some students with mental handicaps. It would be more helpful to say, "People are nice to you if you are nice to them."

- The counselor should establish a degree of structure within the group and adhere to fixed behavioral and time limits. Off-task behaviors should be confronted in a friendly but firm manner.
- The counselor should be familiar with and able to employ a variety of verbal and nonverbal procedures when counseling students with mental handicaps.

Counseling students with mental handicaps can prove challenging to even the best prepared and most empathic facilitator. In addition to their intellectual limitations and difficulties with abstract reasoning, many mentally handicapped students are characterized by a lack of motivation toward independence and achievement, which carries over into the counseling process. Some children are aggressive and restless. Coping with their short attention span and maladaptive behavior patterns may require a great deal of patience and creativity by the counselor.

Group procedures are usually more effective than individual approaches with mentally handicapped students (Bello, 1989). Impairment in adaptive behavior is a primary difficulty of the retarded; a group situation provides an environment for the student to practice social behaviors. Another advantage of a group setting concerns the opportunity to interact with and gain the acceptance of peers. Through peer interaction, students can develop alternative ways of coping with problems as well as learn how to give and receive emotional support. Finally, observing a student in a group situation provides the counselor with a diagnostic tool for making recommendations to teachers and for determining whether or not a more individualized counseling approach is needed.

Most research on group counseling with mentally handicapped individuals has shown directive approaches to be more effective than non-directive techniques (Humes & Suggs, 1988). The role of the counselor may need to include such functions as introducing topics, keeping the group on task, encouraging participation, and imposing behavioral limitations. In many cases, the counselor may need to be actively engaged in teaching particular skills, while at the same time offering support and encouragement for the student's attempts in coping with his or her problems. Role playing is an effective tool in helping students with mental handicaps learn appropriate ways of acting in social situations. Other techniques that do not rely heavily on verbal skills and have been found particularly useful include activity group counseling, simulation games, and art education/therapy.

Counseling Students with Visual Impairments

In general, traditional counseling approaches based on verbal interaction are as effective with students with visual impairments as they are with sighted people. However, the counselor will need to make some adjustment in the counseling process to accommodate some students' reduced ability to communicate nonverbally and to adjust for differences in terms of counseling needs and expectations.

It is important that the counselor be sensitive to environmental cues that have particular meanings for students with severe visual impairments. Because they cannot observe nonverbal messages that communicate the emotional status of others, these students have learned to rely heavily on auditory cues. Their level of psychological comfort in the counseling situation may be affected by the efforts that the counselor makes to establish rapport. Most students with visual impairments are accustomed to structured activity and may be more comfortable, particularly in initial sessions, with highly structured situations. Thus, a question-answer format may be a more appropriate way to initiate counseling than an open-ended format in which the student is encouraged to volunteer feelings.

Group counseling has been used extensively with people who are blind (Johnson, 1989), and it appears to be a particularly appropriate technique to cope with the problem areas that most frequently concern students with visual impairments. As with individual counseling, group methods will require some major adjustments because of the reduced amount of nonverbal communication available. Students may be reluctant to speak in groups for fear of talking at the same time as another member. Silence, too, may pose problems for the counselor since nonverbal means of encouraging a student to speak are not available. The solution that many counselors have adopted is to structure the groups in such a way that long silences and two people speaking at the same time do not occur. Some group leaders prefer to direct the discussion and call upon members who appear ready to speak. Others use a co-therapist to help keep closer contact with the group interaction and bridge silence gaps by talking with each other. Sometimes, however, it seems that such methods are devised primarily to facilitate the comfort of the counselor rather than that of the students. If the counselor can overcome his or her own discomfort and allow a sense of humor to penetrate the group session, many of the problems will disappear.

If alternative communication strategies such as role playing, peer facilitation, and bibliotherapy are used to augment verbal interaction, benefits are likely to be even greater. Role playing allows blind and sighted students to act out their responses to each other in an effort to understand underlying feelings and thoughts. Bibliotherapy can be used with students of all ages to help them adjust to blindness and reorient their concept of self through identification with fictional or nonfictional others (Roberts, 1984).

Counseling Students with Hearing Impairments

Communication difficulties represent the most profound and pervasive barrier to effective counseling with hearing impaired persons. From the deaf student's standpoint, the problems are threefold, involving speech, language, and conceptual limitations. From the counselor's perspective, additional difficulties are encountered in attempting to respond in a language that the student can understand.

Most students who are deaf were born with their hearing loss or acquired it before they learned to talk or use language. Consequently, the vast majority of deaf students are unable to communicate orally in a way that is easily intelligible to people outside their immediate family. Likewise, most students who are deaf, particularly those who were prelingually deafened, have difficulty with speechreading. Few people fully understand the limitations of speechreading. In actuality, 40–60% of the sounds in the English language look just like some other sound on the lips. Numerous interferences such as poor lighting, mustaches, and head movements further reduce the speech that can be lipread to about 20 to 30%. The language difficulties of deaf students are additionally manifested in poor reading ability and underdeveloped vocabulary which, in turn, levy limitations on the counseling process (Vernon & Andrews, 1990).

Manual communication (finger spelling and sign language) is the method of communication preferred by most people who are deaf. **Successful counseling with nonverbal students requires that the counselor be proficient in sign language.**

The fact that the vast majority of school counselors have had **no** training in sign language represents a discouraging aspect of counseling students who are deaf, and it is a problem with no easy solution. Although rudimentary skills are easily attained, proficiency would involve learning hundreds of signs, including idioms and different expressions of syntax and grammar.

Nonverbal students will often require the use of interpreters in mainstreamed school situations. The interpreters themselves may be able to provide the counselor with information that will facilitate communication. Although the presence and involvement of a third person is certainly not ideal in a counseling situation, there may be instances in which it is unavoidable. Some suggestions for using interpreters follow:

- Whenever possible, follow the student's preferences in choice of interpreters. The use of parents or other close relative may inhibit communication in counseling sessions and should be avoided if the student requests.
- Seat everyone within comfortable visual range of each other, but place the student closest to you to reinforce your primary interest in him or her. Address the student directly.
- Request that the interpreter verbalize what is being manually communicated.
- Never develop or allow the interpreter to initiate side conversations about the student in his or her presence.

In the event that the student and his or her family do not have access to interpreters, the counselor can help by making initial contacts. A list of interpreters in the local community can be obtained from the National Registry of Interpreters, Wisconsin School for the Deaf, Delevan, Wisconsin.

Counseling with students who are deaf or hard of hearing is one of the most neglected areas in the literature of both special education and counseling. Virtually no research exists that clearly delineates counseling strategies or theoretical models that are appropriate for hearing impaired people, particularly those who are prelingually deaf. A major task of the counselor may involve breaking down barriers of mistrust and suspicion and helping deaf and hard of hearing students develop skills and motivation to cope with their problems in an independent fashion. To accomplish these goals, the counselor must be willing to depart from traditional verbal encounters and focus on highly concrete experiences.

One of the most effective counseling techniques for students who are hearing impaired is role playing. Because it can be employed nonverbally, role playing can be used as a method of eliciting problems and for working through solutions. It can be used in group situations to help students develop and practice social skills or to learn means of handling job interviews. It can also be used in individual counseling such as acting out situations in which a student learns to cope with others who tease and taunt.

SPECIALIZED APPROACHES TO COUNSELING STUDENTS WITH DISABILITIES

On the following pages are descriptions of three alternatives to the traditional counseling methodologies that are employed by most school counselors. Bibliotherapy, role playing, and creative arts/activity counseling are not presented as preferred methods of communicating with students with handicaps, nor is it suggested that these approaches are more appropriate for handicapped than for nonhandicapped students. These specialized methods are presented as approaches that share several characteristics: they rely heavily on individual responsibility; they focus on **doing** more than **discussing**; they foster creativity, cooperation, and commitment to a task; and they contain built-in mechanisms to help a student learn personal and interpersonal skills.

Bibliotherapy

Taken from the Greek words **biblion** (book) and **therapeio** (healing), bibliotherapy is the use of books to produce affective change and to promote personality growth & development. Although the healing power of reading has been acknowledged through the ages, the concept of bibliotherapy as a formal therapeutic strategy is a product of the 20th century. First used as an isolated form of treatment for mentally ill patients, bibliotherapy gained stature as a result of a series of studies conducted at the Menninger Clinic in Topeka, Kansas, during the 1930s. Since that time, bibliotherapy has become an accepted form of counseling at numerous hospitals and psychiatric clinics, with librarians and physicians cooperating in treatment.

The use of bibliotherapy in educational and other nonmedical settings is a relatively recent occurrence. Experimental research concerning its value as a means of changing behavior or attitudes has been mixed (Lenkowsky, 1987; Riordan & Wilson, 1989), but it is becoming increasingly popular and is often recommended as an adjunct to more traditional forms of counseling. Some of the advantages of bibliotherapy include:

- With appropriate modifications, bibliotherapy can be used with students of all ages. Differences in reading levels can be accommodated through careful selection of materials and/or through oral reading by the counselor or teacher. Students who are visually impaired can participate because of the wide availability of large print and talking books.
- Bibliotherapy can be used with children individually, in small groups, or in classroom situations. The differential needs and interests of students can be met simultaneously. Thus, the counselor can help students cope with common developmental problems relating to their disability, while nonhandicapped students can be assisted in the development of positive attitudes.
- Little formal training or experience is required to become a creative and skilled bibliotherapist. Counselors can train teachers or student helpers to read and lead group discussions, thus allowing the bibliotherapeutic process to be used with a large number of students.
- Bibliotherapy can be used as either a preventive or a remedial approach with children, and it can be an effective technique with a wide array of student problems or concerns.

Bibliotherapy helps the reader by the processes of **identification, catharsis,** and **insight.** When a student is able to see the feelings, problems, or life experiences of a literary character as being in some way similar to his or her own, identification with that character occurs and may extend to identification with real people. The process of identification helps the reader gain an understanding of the universality of human experiences; in terms of students with disabilities, this affiliation through literature can be the first step in reducing the perception of them as essentially different from nonhandicapped people. Catharsis occurs for the reader as he or she vicariously experiences the emotions of the literary character. As students empathize with the fictional hero, they are able to purge their own feelings of frustration, anger, grief, or other emotions. The release of psychological tension that occurs is therapeutic in itself, although the benefits of catharsis are generally temporary. Insight is a cognitive experience that can occur most fruitfully after catharsis and emotional release have been obtained. When readers have achieved identification and experienced emotional release through catharsis, they can then examine their own problems, feelings, or attitudes in a more objective light, paving the way for problem solving or behavioral change.

Guidelines for Conducting Bibliotherapy

Like all counseling strategies, the success of bibliotherapy depends upon the care with which it is implemented. The counselor can help insure that students benefit from the process by adhering to some specific guidelines. First, **reading materials should be carefully selected.** Not only must the counselor have read the book or story that is to be used, but he or she must carefully evaluate it both in terms of the quality of the literature and of specific student characteristics. Regarding the literature itself, the primary criterion is its ability to provide identification with the characters. The counselor should examine the material in terms of its accuracy, possible emotional impact, readability, length, and general plot. At the same time, the counselor should be knowledgeable of student factors such as age, sex, problems, reading level, and interests before suggesting a particular selection. The counselor must be familiar with physical limitations of students that would require special reading materials or aids.

Reading should be supplemented by discussion, counseling, or both. Whether bibliotherapy is used with an individual student who is undergoing a serious problem or as a classroom approach to the development of positive attitudes toward people with handicaps, the students should follow their reading with a discussion of their reactions to the material. The counselor and student(s) might focus on a discussion of the behavior and experience of a character in light of the student's perceptions, the feelings and thoughts generated in the student by the story, or specific situations in the literature that provoked agreement or disagreement by the student. Follow-up need not be limited to discussion between the counselor and an individual student. The creative counselor can use a variety of activities that will help students internalize their feelings and explore the reactions of others to the same event. Developing role plays, holding panel discussions, creating different story endings, using puppets to enact scenes, and designing murals represent some of the many ways that student interest and involvement can be continued.

The counselor must recognize the limitations of bibliotherapy. Like all counseling strategies, bibliotherapy is not appropriate for everyone. Some students, instead of achieving insight when reading, may tend to rationalize or intellectualize their problems. Others may expect too much from reading; instead of providing a stimulus for problem solving, some students may expect a book to offer instantaneous solutions. There are some students whose past failures with reading have become so ingrained that they will resist participating, even when stories are read orally by others. Some people simply do not like literature and are unable to identify with fictional characters.

Literally thousands of books are commercially available to help children and adolescents cope with problems and understand the lives of others. The screening of books can be an awesome task. Fortunately, excellent bibliographies are frequently published in journals and can be used by the counselor or librarian to determine book selection.

Role Playing

Role playing, a derivative of the psychodramatic techniques introduced by Moreno (1964), is a method in which problems and situations are acted out by an individual or by a group. Although role playing has been used extensively in hospitals and clinics to foster awareness of self and others and to modify attitudes and behaviors, its use in school counseling situations has been limited.

Advantages of Role Playing

Role playing offers a number of advantages:

- It gives the student an opportunity to express different types of behaviors and attitudes with a minimum of personal threat.
- Acting helps to bring out the conflicts, feelings, fears, and wishes that the student may not be able to verbalize.
- Assuming a role that is different from one's own can help the student develop an understanding and acceptance of a variety of viewpoints.
- Role playing gives the student a chance to demonstrate what he or she would actually do rather than merely discussing what one might do.
- It provides opportunities for introducing a variety of roles and experiences into the student's world within a short period of time.
- In a group situation, the audience has an opportunity to observe a number of different responses to a given problem or situation.
- Threatening situations can be re-created and acted out by the

counselor, giving the student a chance to experiment with different types of responses.

In addition to the general benefits just listed, role playing can be a particularly useful means to cope with problems experienced by students with disabilities. From a practical standpoint, role playing offers a technique that is not as dependent upon verbal interactions as are many forms of counseling. Students who may be limited in language and social experiences can use role playing to learn new social skills and to express personal problems. Omizo, Hershberger, & Omizo (1988) found that learning disabled and emotionally handicapped students were able to decrease aggressiveness and destructive behaviors as a result of group counseling focusing on role-playing. Jaret (1987) established structured role playing sessions to reduce stress in troubled children. Goldstein and Strain (1988) used role-playing to increase positive interaction between handicapped and non-handicapped students.

The Process of Role Playing

One of the advantages of role playing is its flexibility in structure and its adaptability to a wide variety of situations. It can be used in individual counseling, as a type of behavior rehearsal to desensitize the client to anxiety-provoking situations. The counselor may participate in a dialogue to help the student see another point of view. It is most often used in groups, but even then, role playing can be structured differently to accommodate the size of the group and the needs of the students. In a group situation, either multiple or single group role-playing procedures can be used. In multiple group role playing, the entire group participates, simultaneously acting out situations in subgroups. This procedure is most effective when it is desirable for all members of the group to try out new behaviors. It is a useful way to compare different responses since the roles are the same for each group. It is also an effective way to reduce shyness and self-consciousness of students since an audience is not observing. Multiple group role playing is an effective technique to help large numbers of students practice social or employability skills or to experiment with concerns that are common to the group, such as parent-child conflicts.

When the primary purpose is to develop sensitivity to the feelings of others, the single group role playing procedure may be more effective. In this method, one group acts out the situation while the remaining members observe. Although playing a role before an audience can make an individual self-conscious, this situation may be desirable. The actor may become sensitized to his or her own behavior and become more consciously aware of behavioral errors. The members of the audience serve an important analytical function in single group role plays. They can point out, from an objective standpoint, the effects of one actor's behavior on another and can frequently trace the chain of events that led to different attitudes and responses by the various actors.

The process of role playing includes four broad steps: identification of the specific problem to be enacted, delineation of the various roles, dramatization of the situation, and follow-up discussion. The identification of the problem may be generated informally, as a logical outcome of a group discussion or an individual counseling session. In many cases, the counselor may choose to announce the given situation as part of a planned guidance strategy, such as concerns with attitudes toward students with disabilities. In order to clarify the problem, the counselor may wish to lead a brief discussion of the topic and to encourage group members to share personal experiences that illustrate the problem. Thus, students with disabilities may describe situations in which they have been ignored, patronized, or stared at in public places and request help in responding to such behaviors. Nonhandicapped students may discuss their discomfort in the presence of individuals who are disabled and express anxiety at being unsure as to how or whether to offer assistance. Any student may be likely to mention problems concerned with accepting criticism of others, dealing with **put-downs,** insecurity in social situations, or resolving conflicts with teachers or parents.

Once the problem area is clarified, the counselor should establish a scene to be enacted and assign specific roles. If the role playing is part of a planned program, roles can be written out on cards for the players. The students should have enough information to enable them to act out a particular behavior or situation but not so much that they will feel compelled to delete their own personalities from the acting. It is sometimes helpful to allow the players several minutes to assimilate their role and prepare to enact certain behaviors. This period of time can be used to prepare the audience for their observation tasks. They might be directed to watch the behaviors of the role players and to attempt to decipher feelings that go unexpressed. They should attempt to note the effects of one actor's behavior on others and to determine whether or not the players' behaviors appear to accurately reflect their feelings.

In general, the more natural and spontaneous the acting, the more that real-life behaviors and attitudes will emerge. In some cases, the scene will not come to a natural close, and the counselor may need to step in and conclude the dialogue. At other times, the play may falter because of the actors' conflicts with each other in playing the scene. In such instances, the counselor may need to intervene and allow the players and observers to process the situation before continuing.

After the role play has been concluded, the actors can discuss the dynamics of the interaction, expressing their feelings toward playing a given role and their reactions to the others on stage. Then the observers could offer opinions regarding the interaction, pointing out instances in which the players appeared uncomfortable and the effect that certain words or behaviors had on the audience. If a debate ensues regarding a particular behavior and its effect on the outcome of the problem situation, the counselor may wish to repeat the process, allowing new participants to enact the scene with different behaviors.

Creative Arts and Activities in Counseling

Another approach that has been found to be particularly useful with handicapped students involves the use of creative arts, games, and activities in counseling. As with bibliotherapy and role playing, activity-oriented approaches rely on the use of **props** as a means of involving the student. Attention is focused on the interaction of the student and given task, activity, or creative undertaking. When used in a group setting, the additional dimensions of interpersonal relationships, cooperation, and teamwork are included.

Art and Music in Counseling

Art is one medium that is suitable for almost all children, regardless of handicap. Art is capable of satisfying many of the emotional needs of children and of teaching the concepts that form the basis of learning. Art helps children master their environment and produce something tangible, fostering social communicability and self-concept. Art challenges a child's imagination and decision-making processes, and helps in the development of communication skills, self-confidence, and independence (Eydenberg, 1986). Making pictures is one way that a handicapped child can describe his or her world, and it fulfills a need to share thoughts and ideas. If the learning environment is accepting and free, the child will explain his or her creations as they progress.

Contrary to the fears of many counselors, artistic talent is not a prerequisite to incorporate art into counseling strategies. Imagination is a helpful characteristic as is the interest and cooperation of the school's art instructor, but the counselor who lacks these aids can find assistance in a variety of helpful books.

The value of music as an integral part of the education, training, and therapy of handicapped children has been recognized for a number of years. Appropriate use of music can improve children's speech, help regain the use of limbs, improve the sense of rhythm, and calm tense bodies. Dance, in particular, has been successful in building self-esteem and relationships, as well as motor coordination. It is suggested as the treatment of choice for children with motor disabilities and those with attention deficits (Lasseter, Privette, Brown, and Duer, 1989).

As with art, the school counselor need not be gifted to incorporate music into his or her counseling program. The availability of a wide range of music on records and tapes insures easy accessibility and allows the counselor to participate in activities with the children. For whatever specific purpose it is used, the basic principle behind music therapy is the freedom of personal expression and interpretation. Music creates an atmosphere of comfort in which students feel free to express themselves, orally or in movement, without fear of failure or criticism. In such an environment, the counselor can help children learn concepts that carry over to other aspects of their education. Instruction in science, history, or language arts can be facilitated by accompanying music, as can auditory and visual discrimination skills. In addition, music can be used for its tranquilizing effect on agitated or hyperactive youngsters, or it can be used as a reward for appropriate social behavior.

Play and Activities in Counseling

For all young children, play is important. But for children with certain handicaps, it may be especially valuable. Play can assist in the remediation of problems that involve language, visual and auditory perception, gross and fine motor skills, short attention span, hyperactivity, and distractibility. Further, play is the child's natural medium of self-expression. Many children with disabilities have difficulty in verbalizing and conceptualizing what is occurring in their minds and bodies. Play provides the child with the freedom to act out experiences and to master reality by experimenting and planning. Axline (1976) identified guidelines for counselors engaged in play therapy:

- develop a warm, friendly relationship
- accept the child as he or she is
- establish feelings of permissiveness
- recognize and reflect feelings
- respect the child's ability to solve his or her own problems
- do not direct the child's actions or conversation
- do not hurry the play process
- establish necessary behavioral limitations

For older children, **play therapy** may be more appropriately called **activity therapy,** and the process may incorporate more group interaction and verbal interchange. Students with disabilities often respond positively to structured games such as those suggested in books of experiential activities. However, counseling that uses activity as its medium does not have to rely on structured games. Task-oriented projects can be developed around craft projects, creative writing, physical education, or other curricular areas. The focus of activity counseling is on **learning through doing,** although the process of counseling, including acceptance, sharing, and feedback, remains the same as in traditional counseling.

Guidelines for counselors concerning activity groups include the following:

- The atmosphere of the group should be democratic rather than authoritarian or permissive.
- Group cohesiveness is more likely to develop when the tone of the group is based on an attitude of mutual help and encouragement.
- The group leader should be an active participant, serving both as a facilitator and a model.
- With some training, groups can be led by parents, teachers, paraprofessionals, or student peer facilitators.
- Group size can vary according to the objectives and activities involved.
- A mix of sexes and personalities stimulates productive interaction and personal growth.

Group counseling based on creative arts and activities has many variations. In spite of differences in media and techniques, the various approaches share several characteristics. They are fun and nonthreatening; they are helpful in building self-esteem and social skills; they emphasize **action** and de-emphasize **talking;** and they build on the concept of play and creativity as recognized human needs.

Chapter Five

CAREER GUIDANCE FOR STUDENTS WITH DISABILITIES

Wherever and however it is accomplished, for most people work is the single most influential element in their environment. A person's self-concept is often highly intertwined with the feelings he or she has about work. For most people, work represents their livelihood; it is, therefore, greatly responsible for their standard of living, life-style, and leisure activities. In short, work is an integral part of identity.

Documented statistics, news reports, and personal observation all speak loudly to the damage effected when young people are ill-prepared to play productive roles in the world of work. Career education is important for **all** students, but it is particularly vital for pupils with disabilities. Some special educators have long responded to the need by developing sheltered workshops, instituting occupational information courses, and joining forces with vocational rehabilitation efforts to establish work-study programs. However, large-scale efforts to address the need for career education for students with disabilities were begun only during the past decade.

The 1980s were undoubtedly the landmark years in terms of addressing long-recognized needs for more adequate and appropriate career education for handicapped individuals, and the effects of various efforts are increasingly visible. The recently enacted Americans With Disabilities Act supports previous legislation which was designed to end discrimination in the work place.

In spite of the tremendous strides that have been made, however, statistics concerning the career education and employment of special students remain grim. For example:

- The vast majority of students with disabilities leave school without salable skills (Levinson, 1986).
- Unemployment rates among disabled adults range from 50 to 80 percent (Ehrsten and Izzo, 1988).

81

- Most employed disabled men and women are placed in unskilled, manual jobs (Roessler, 1987).

The responsibility for such appalling statistics must be shared. Special educators know little about career development, and vocational educators are generally unfamiliar with the needs of students with disabilities. Further, specialists have failed to work together to combine resources and improve services (Halpern, 1985).

School counselors are ill-prepared to counsel people with disabilities regarding career decisions (Chubon, 1985). Most counselors have had no training in special education and have had limited vocational exposure beyond formal course work.

Parents frequently have lower expectations of their children than the disability dictates; overprotection can prevent children from learning about the world of work through home responsibilities, visits within the community, and other natural experiences.

People with disabilities have contributed to their own lack of vocational success. By allowing themselves to remain dependent upon their families, by not seeking out academic, social, and career challenges, and by not assuming responsibility for their own futures, people with disabilities prevent themselves from developing salable skills, and they reinforce society's view of them as helpless and dependent.

COUNSELOR RESPONSIBILITIES IN CAREER EDUCATION

An important issue in the career education of students with disabilities concerns the responsibilities of various professional personnel. Considering the wide range of competencies needed to develop and implement a comprehensive career education program, no one individual or professional group could be expected to undertake the tasks. Ideally, such responsibilities are shared by all members of a school staff in addition to the student, his or her family, and community organizations.

The guidance and counseling activities involved in the various phases of career education will require counselors who can:

- Conduct formal and informal career assessment as an integral part of an overall assessment program.
- Design and implement career exploration activities.
- Develop and use community resources.

- Consult with parents concerning the career development of their children.
- Consult with other educators concerning the development of self-awareness and decision-making skills in students.
- Work with handicapped students in the selection of training opportunities and job possibilities.
- Carry out individual and group counseling with handicapped students on an ongoing basis (Jenkins, 1987; Kanchier, 1990).

As competencies and responsibilities are defined more specifically, it becomes increasingly apparent that the tasks involved in the career development of disabled students are numerous, complex, and impossible to conduct through a single professional role. As an example, the knowledge and attitudes necessary for the accomplishment of a single component of career education -placement- include the following: (a) a functional understanding of the student's values and needs regarding work, (b) knowledge of occupational psychology and the sociological aspects of work in our culture, (c) knowledge of present and future occupational trends and fluctuations, (d) awareness of counselors' own values and needs regarding work, (e) understanding of particular placement problems of students with specific disabilities, (f) awareness of counselors' own inadequacies and prejudices concerning specific disability groups, (g) confidence in disabled workers, and (h) a functional level of self-confidence in the selective placement of clients. This list does not include the various **skills** that counselors must employ during the placement process!

VOCATIONAL CHARACTERISTICS OF STUDENTS WITH SPECIFIC DISABILITIES

Disabled students share many vocational characteristics with the general population. Ideas about work are transmitted through the family; the value of education, the role of work in the establishment of one's identity, and concepts of responsibility and independence are functions of socioeconomic factors rather than the presence of a disability. However, people with handicaps do share among themselves certain characteristics and needs that set them apart from the general population and establish areas of commonality among all forms of disability. For example, people with disabilities share the burden of discrimination in the marketplace.

They commonly experience the anger and frustration that comes from coping with never-ending physical barriers and problems with transportation or communication. They share the problems associated with underemployment, continued financial dependence, and inadequate vocational training.

Although disabled students share numerous characteristics, problems, and needs with their nondisabled peers as well as with the general **handicapped** population, members of different disability groups appear to have some vocational characteristics and needs that warrant their treatment as separate populations.

Characteristics of Students with Mental Handicaps

Of the 2.4 million retarded individuals under the age of 21 in the United States, 75% could be fully self-supporting, given appropriate education and training (McLeod, 1985). The fact that the majority are not self-sufficient appears to be related to a number of factors.

One problem concerns common misconceptions regarding the types of jobs that people who are retarded can accomplish. Many individuals, including educators and employers, believe that retarded people can succeed only in routine, repetitive, and simple jobs. Recent research, however, has amply demonstrated that many individuals with mental handicaps can learn extremely complex tasks given appropriate and sufficient training. Even severely disabled individuals have learned complicated manual skills such as assembling a drill machine or bicycle brakes. Well trained mentally handicapped adults have been shown to be able to find and keep jobs (Kanchier, 1990).

Another area of misunderstanding concerns the aspirations of retarded individuals. Many professionals have assumed that career and vocational training for retarded students is complicated by the fact that they hold either too high or too low vocational aspirations and are, therefore, doomed to failure. However, research has shown that retarded students' career expectations are realistic.

To date, the lack of training available for most retarded persons has contributed to their vocational problems. Although personal-social factors have been found to be the most important determinants of the employability of retarded people, few educational programs have emphasized the development of these skills. Instead, public school programs have focused almost exclusively on the attainment of academic skills. A shift is necessary in order to more appropriately meet their vocational needs. First, an emphasis should be placed on the attainment of personal-social skills such as courtesy, cleanliness, punctuality, cooperation, and responsibility. The development of such skills can be accomplished through a variety of methods, including classroom instruction and counseling. Role playing and behavior modification are two techniques that have been found to be very effective in the development of personal-social skills; each provides a protected but structured environment for practice of new behaviors. Secondly, educational programs for retarded students need a greater emphasis on work experience. Public schools that have initiated work-study programs have met with success, particularly in terms of enhancing the employability of students.

Characteristics of Students with Visual Impairments

The rate of unemployment among adults who are blind is extremely high, with figures generally estimated to range between 40 and 50% (Dixon, 1983). Those who are employed have been unable to find work in a wide range of occupations, with most surveys showing that more than half of the males are employed in 11–13 jobs, while the majority of females found work in 8–10 occupations.

It has often been assumed that much of the employment difficulty of people with severe visual impairment is due to a high incidence of vocational immaturity among the population. It has been suggested that blind children are more externally controlled than their sighted peers, a condition that leads to vocational apathy. Parental overprotection, a lack of opportunity to watch people at work, and limited experience with work-like tasks have all been cited as factors contributing to the vocational immaturity of visually impaired students. This has been particularly true of girls, who have been raised to be passive, sheltered, and dependent (Koestler, 1983). Undoubtedly, a significant element in the problem has concerned the attitudes of employers, who have demonstrated in numerous studies their lack of confidence in visually impaired workers.

Another problem that appears to plague students with visual impairment, particularly those who are adventitiously blind, concerns their adjustment to the disability. While the topic of adjustment is covered elsewhere and will not be explored in this chapter, it is important to remember that the problem can permeate every aspect of a student's life, including vocational development. Vocational rehabilitation counselors often report that as clients near completion of a training program, they frequently react negatively to the anticipated stress of acting independently within a sighted world. The clients often respond by regressing to an unrealistic and unattainable vocational goal, criticizing the program for lack of appropriate training, and ultimately refusing to work at all. Before originating specific career planning activities, the counselor needs to assess the student's level of personal adjustment and, if necessary, help the student reach a level of self-acceptance that will permit him or her to begin to think and plan realistically for the future.

For students with no functional vision, employability will be largely dependent upon the development of several basic personal and social skills. First, it is essential that the student become adept in terms of mobility and orientation. In the event that the student has not developed these skills, the counselor can help by contacting local or state agencies that are equipped to provide training.

The development of appropriate posture, gait, and other nonverbal mannerisms will be vital to the visually handicapped person entering the employment arena. Postural habits common in visually impaired people include rocking, head bobbing, eye rubbing, and arm flaying. While the habits may serve the purpose of reducing tension and can, therefore, be beneficial to blind persons, chances of social and vocational success are greater if the mannerisms are avoided in public.

Since facial expressions are generally learned through visual imitation, many blind students are deficient in this area and will need to be systematically taught. Because sighted people sometimes interpret the "silent" faces of blind persons as disinterest or boredom, career success within a sighted world can be enhanced if visually handicapped students learn some rudimentary skills of nonverbal communication.

Other personal skills that blind students will need to concentrate on more fully than their sighted peers include grooming habits, such as hair care, makeup application, and clothes matching. They may need practice in telephone dialing, money identification, or socially acceptable eating skills. The counselor can assist by stressing the importance of such skills in social and work situations, by working with the student and his or her parents to review and practice methods, and by providing instructional resource materials.

Characteristics of Students With Hearing Impairments

Under favorable conditions, deaf and severely hearing impaired people have repeatedly demonstrated their ability to succeed in a wide variety of professional and blue-collar occupations. Deaf workers are consistently reported to be highly stable workers, and typical employer evaluations characterize them as being equal or superior to hearing employees in terms of job performance, safety records, attendance, health conditions, punctuality, dependability, and motivation.

In spite of demonstrated success of people who are deaf at all levels of employment, statistical data reveal a wide gap between possibilities and reality. Among deaf adults, underemployment is a more prevalent problem than unemployment. The great majority of the employed deaf population are engaged in manual labor, and most are confined to jobs in several specific occupations, such as printing and dry cleaning.

The majority of deaf persons, including many of above-average intelligence and ability, are trapped in routine, unchallenging jobs with no opportunity for advancement. Additionally, students with severe hearing impairment themselves hold mistaken ideas regarding careers and do not identify with aspiring or successful workers. These generalized characteristics of people with hearing impairments lead to descriptions of various career guidance needs of students:

- **Deaf students need information and experience related to social habits and customs.** Deaf workers are often unaware of and insensitive to their own impact on others; they may display asocial behavior such as calling employers by nicknames or asking extremely personal questions.
- **Deaf students need realistic information about jobs and job requirements.** Lack of information about various occupations is a major contribution to the limited choice of careers. Information about the world of work is passed from older students to younger ones, a network that is often independent of general school and familial influences.
- **Deaf students need comprehensive career counseling.** Career counseling should focus on developing skills for daily living, social competence, independence, and higher aspiration levels, as well as vocational preparation.
- **Deaf students need skills in seeking employment.** The most difficult

vocational tasks for deaf workers are locating jobs, completing job applications, and interviewing.

- **Deaf students need practice in goal setting, planning ahead, making decisions, and problem solving.** According to employers, these difficulties are responsible for the failure of many deaf people to advance in jobs.

Fortunately, career education for deaf students is enhanced by a number of current trends and the invention of new technology. Interpreter services, for example, have increased dramatically during the past decade; training opportunities in interpreting and other support services are offered by increasing numbers of institutions of higher learning.

Characteristics of Students With Physical Disabilities

Because of the sheer number and the diverse nature of the many disabilities associated with orthopedic, neuromuscular, or chronic health problems, it is difficult to isolate vocational characteristics and needs that are generally associated with physically disabled students. Considerable research has been conducted with certain populations, such as people with traumatic spinal cord injuries, and results have been consistent enough to draw some conclusions about that specific group. When generalizing results to other physically handicapped populations, however, cautious interpretation is in order. Hence, the discussion concerning the vocational guidance needs and characteristics of students with physical disabilities must be general in nature. It is important to remember to consider each student as an individual whose characteristics and needs are, for the most, unique.

As with all areas of disability, various characteristics associated with a physical condition will have some degree of impact upon career decision making. It is especially important that the counselor become well acquainted with the etiology and characteristics of the particular disabilities represented by students within the school.

One of the primary vocational difficulties faced by people with orthopedic or neuromuscular difficulties concerns physical barriers. These barriers impact upon all aspects of life and affect such diverse areas as family travel, choice of schools and programs, job transportation, and urban vs. rural living. The following are illustrative of the diverse ways in which physical barriers affect the career education of students with disabilities:

- Because of the difficulties in revamping facilities, orthopedically handicapped students are frequently bused many miles to a single barrier-free school. Because of the distances involved, parent education programs, extracurricular activities, work-study programs, and career exploration groups are often severely curtailed or completely eliminated.
- Physically handicapped people frequently require an attendant, someone to assist with activities such as personal hygiene, eating, or study. Colleges and employers are not legally required to provide attendant care, forcing many students to forego plans or seek care at great personal expense.

THE CAREER DEVELOPMENT PROCESS

It is helpful to look at student progression through career education in terms of four phases: career awareness, career exploration, career preparation, and career placement. Given appropriate educational and support services, most disabled students would ideally be able to move smoothly through the various career development stages, acquiring appropriate competencies as they progress. In actuality, the pace may be slower for many students with disabilities and some may move back and forth among the various stages. Many students with disabilities will not have had adequate social or self-development experiences to enable them to achieve various career awareness competencies while in elementary school. Others will take longer to reach the career placement phase because of difficulties in skill development directly or indirectly associated with their disability. Some students will exhibit the characteristics and needs associated with a specific handicapping condition and will thus show uneven or slow progress through the various stages. The majority of disabled students will probably rely more than do their nonhandicapped peers on the assistance of counselors and other school personnel in order to attain their career development goals.

Career Awareness and Exploration

During the elementary years, the primary focus of career education should be on two broad areas: knowledge of occupations and introduction to work concepts. Both goals are approached from an introductory and broad-based standpoint, with general awareness being the desired outcome.

In many cases, guidance activities can be designed that are broad enough in scope that they cover both of the career awareness goals and involve the three main elements of learning: attitudes, information, and self-understanding.

One of the goals of the career awareness phase of a career education program is to introduce the child to a variety of occupations. Structured activities for this purpose are particularly important for handicapped children who have had limited opportunities to develop familiarity with occupations through family outings. Blind children, for example, are less likely than sighted students to use visits to stores and restaurants to become aware of the many occupations represented by adults. Because of the difficulties associated with mobility, orthopedically handicapped children generally have limited exposure to the world beyond home, school, and treatment center. Retarded children may not be aware that people **helping** in stores, amusement parks, or other places are actually **working** unless systematic instructional efforts are made.

Elementary school children need more than factual information about occupations; they also need to explore various work-oriented concepts in order to gain a better understanding of themselves in relation to work. Several concepts that are appropriate for children in K to 6 programs include **work has dignity; work means different things to different people; work has different rewards or satisfactions;** and **education and work are interrelated.**

Research has repeatedly shown that social skills are a vital factor in career success, yet children are seldom systematically taught communication behaviors. Normal play and social interaction with peers and adults often result in the awareness of the relationship between certain behaviors and consequences. Thus, many children learn informally that their own attitudes and behaviors are related to their social and academic success. However, handicapped children have little opportunity for such informal learning. The restriction of their peer interaction or the tendency for others to treat them differently often precludes their exposure to the rough and tumble learning process that many children experience.

Structured opportunities for skill building in social interaction can be incorporated into ongoing classroom activities or provided through small group exercises. Children can easily be taught and encouraged to use appropriate feedback techniques during classroom discussions and projects.

During the exploratory stage of career development, the individual's self-concept evolves in relation to the world of work. Students need to begin relating their own abilities, needs, and interests to possible future roles in work and leisure activities. Self-examination and occupational exploration through part-time jobs can facilitate the career exploration process.

Traditional means of helping students explore the world of work at this level include student participation in jobs inside and outside of the classroom, visits to the class by resource persons, and field trips. Work-study programs have been particularly successful with some handicapped students (Ehrsten & Izzo, 1988). Significant changes within education are increasingly suggested as being necessary if students with disabilities are to really be served. Edgar (1988), for example, maintains that a mentor system can build from the knowledge that a social network is the most influential element in the career decision-making of students with disabilities.

Career Preparation: Assessment of Vocational Interest and Aptitude

The determination of the types of work skills in which a student possesses interest and aptitude is an important component of any career guidance program. Most students begin to develop a sense of their own work-related skills at an early age through play, home chores, and various structured exploratory activities, such as Scouting. Although the student may not associate such tasks with the world of work, most adolescents are able to evaluate their own skills in such broad areas as helping others, working under close supervision, or attention to detail.

Many students with disabilities, however, have little concrete information on which to make self-evaluations. Because of their experiential limitations, it is particularly important that disabled students be provided with various means of assessing vocational interest and aptitude.

Assessment of vocational potential should be made both through ongoing and formal means. Ongoing assessment occurs throughout the student's years in public school and includes the following:

- Assessment of knowledge, interest, and skills through performance in academic classes.
- Evaluation of aptitudes, interests, and achievement in vocational skill courses and other exploratory activities.
- Assessment of work aptitudes and behavior through observation or on-the-job experiences.

Responsibility for the various means of ongoing assessment must be shared among school personnel, as well as with the student and his or her parents. Grades, performance sheets, anecdotal records, and related data can provide important information concerning the general directions in which a student's interests and abilities lie.

Formal assessment of vocational interests is often conducted through standardized inventories such as the **Kuder Occupational Interest Survey** or the **Strong-Campbell Interest Inventory.** Although such instruments were standardized on nondisabled populations, they can provide useful information for many students with disabilities. In some cases, however, such inventories are virtually useless because of too-high reading levels. Fortunately, several interest inventories have been developed for use with special populations, and other have been modified from existing instruments to accommodate particular needs. Several interest/aptitude tests that are frequently used with handicapped students include the following:

- **Career Maturity Inventory (CMI).** The CMI estimates the maturity of a student's attitudes and competencies and determines the need for career advisement. It covers areas such as independence in decision-making and problem-solving abilities.
- **Kuder Preference Record.** Versions of this well-established interest inventory are available for administration orally, in braille, or by tape recording.
- **Picture Interest Exploration Survey (PIES).** The PIES is a kit that requires no reading, is easy to score, and requires no prior familiarity with the world of work.
- **PRG Interest Inventory for the Blind.** This inventory is based on jobs accomplished and hobbies chosen by blind persons. It can be administered orally or by tape recording.
- **Reading-Free Vocational Interest Inventory.** This is a pictorial instru-

ment that requires the student to make one choice from three illustrations. The job areas were chosen from those in which mentally retarded individuals have demonstrated proficiency.

- **Vocational Interest and Sophistication Assessment (VISA).** The VISA is a nonreading, pictorial inventory that was designed to measure the vocational interests of mildly retarded adolescents and adults.
- **Wide-Range Interest-Opinion Test (WRIOT).** The WRIOT measures a wide range of vocational interests. No reading other than **least** and **most** is required; special instructions for severely disabled persons are provided.
- **Work Value Inventory.** This instrument is designed to assess work values concerning career choice and job satisfaction. The reading level is low and the test requires only 20 minutes to complete.

The value of actual work experience as a means of assessing vocational interest and potential is unquestioned. Research indicates that early work experience leads to more stable and successful careers, as well as to more sophisticated vocational development. Actual work experience is a valuable means of helping to determine a student's general potential in areas such as getting along with others, taking orders, or safety procedures, as well as revealing potential for special skill development.

Numerous opportunities are available that enable students with disabilities to obtain a degree of work experience while still in school. One of the most popular and flexible plans is the work-study program, in which students typically work half a day and attend classes half a day. Depending on available resources and individual needs, students with disabilities can be integrated into regular cooperative work programs, placed in programs designed for all students with vocational handicaps, or placed in programs designated for a particular type of impairment. Work stations can be located either at the school or in the community. On-campus placement provides students with the opportunity to learn acceptable work habits in a closely supervised and protected setting. Job experiences might include custodial or janitorial work, serving as a messenger or telephone assistant, or clerical duties. Employment within the community, whether as a volunteer for an agency such as Goodwill Industries, as an intern receiving academic credit, or as a paid, competitive employee, is an excellent way for students to develop and assess their vocational interests, attitudes, and skills. Research has shown that students who participate in work-study programs and after high-school vocational experiences have more job stability and higher earnings (Ehrsten & Izzo, 1988).

Although on-the-job work experience is advocated as an integral part of a vocational exploration plan for students with disabilities, there are some situations in which placement is impossible. In such instances assessment of work potential may need to be accomplished through simulated work experiences. Several of the more common work sample packages include:

- **CLAWSON WORK SAMPLE TEST:** The Clawson was constructed specifically for blind persons. It includes five work samples, two of which are actual job tasks and three which are simulated tasks. They focus on skills requiring dexterity, ranging from gross hand movements to fine finger sensitivity.
- **GENERAL APTITUDE TEST BATTERY (GATB):** The GATB is the most highly researched vocational evaluation instrument in existence. It consists of 12 tests yielding nine aptitudes: intelligence, verbal intelligence, numerical aptitude, spatial aptitude, form perception, clerical perception, motor coordination, finger dexterity, and manual dexterity. A nonverbal version (NATB) is available.
- **JEWISH EMPLOYMENT AND VOCATIONAL SERVICE SYSTEM (JEVS):** This system measures potential in general industrial categories and includes 28 work samples for hands-on assessment of skills, behavior, and interests. Included are such areas as assembly/disassembly, binding, clerical, display and printing, electrical, mail handling, structural development, and metal work.
- **SINGER VOCATIONAL EVALUATION SYSTEM:** This is an audiovisual system with work evaluation in areas such as bench assembly, electrical wiring, plumbing and pipefitting, cooking and baking, and cosmetology.
- **SOCIAL AND PREVOCATIONAL INFORMATION BATTERY (SPIB):** This battery was originally developed for use with mildly retarded people but has been adapted for use with moderately retarded individuals. It includes knowledge tests in the areas of employability, economic self-sufficiency, family living, personal habits, and communication.
- **TESTING, ORIENTATION, AND WORK EVALUATION IN REHABILITATION (TOWER):** This is the oldest and best known work sample evaluation system developed for use with handicapped

people. It consists of 94 work samples clustered into 14 occupational areas. Examples of work samples include jewelry manufacturing, drafting, drawing, sewing, and electronics assembly. Student work habits, work tolerance, attitude, speed, and general motivation are also evaluated.

- **VALPAR COMPONENT WORK SAMPLE SYSTEM:** This test consists of 16 individual assessment units that have been normed on nonhandicapped workers and special disability groups. The 16 areas include skills such as size discrimination, clerical comprehension and aptitude, independent problem solving, eye-hand-foot coordination, and money handling.

The advantages and benefits to students of the work sample approach to vocational assessment have been enumerated by various writers. Among the most frequently cited advantages of work samples are the following:

- They are particularly useful in the evaluation of multihandicapped persons or those with language, educational, or cultural handicaps.
- For many students they provide built-in motivation and reduce test-taking anxiety.
- They evaluate some factors that are difficult to measure with paper and pencil tests, such as ability to follow directions, tool usage, work methods, and initiative.
- They can serve to build self-confidence and feelings of self-esteem in students who have doubted their ability to be successful in any work endeavors.
- They provide a direct, hands-on task that allows the student to perform work and to acquire information about his or her reactions to performing the tasks.
- They can encourage students to begin thinking more seriously about their future.
- They can provide a welcome diversion from traditional verbal activities; some disabled students are more likely to enjoy and succeed in manipulative tasks than in verbal ones.
- They bring reality into the classroom and motivate the student to learn academic and other skills that are related to vocational tasks.

While there are obvious advantages and benefits to using work samples with handicapped students, they do have specific limitations as well (Berkell, 1987; Peterson, 1986). Work samples are restrictive in nature, pertaining only to semiskilled, skilled, or clerical tasks, while neglecting professional and managerial areas. Because of the contrived nature of work samples, performance under actual conditions is not measured. They are not useful for severely disabled individuals. Finally, the systems are usually expensive and may not be cost-effective in consideration of a given school's needs and priorities. In selecting a particular vocational assessment system, the counselor must determine the appropriateness of the programs for the students to be served.

Career and Educational Placement

Regardless of the level of training and degree of vocational skill, handicapped persons generally have difficulty obtaining appropriate employment. In spite of educational and legislative efforts, the situation has not improved in the last decade (Brolin & Gysbers, 1989). The primary cause of the underemployment of disabled workers appears to be related to the attitudes of employers. Studies have repeatedly shown that employers discriminate against handicapped workers and hold unrealistic and irrational opinions regarding their performance on the job.

The facts concerning employability of handicapped workers do not substantiate employers' fears. Several large scale research efforts have concluded:

- There is no effect on insurance costs as a result of hiring disabled workers.
- Most companies report lower absenteeism, lower turnover, and the same or better job performance of handicapped workers.
- Accidents are lower, accommodations are minimal, labor-management cooperation is exceptionally high, and job stability is better than average (Lester & Caudill, 1987).

One recent survey (Eigenbrood & Retish, 1988) revealed that employers who agreed to participate in work experience programs developed positive attitudes toward the students and stated that their participation increased the likelihood they would hire a special education graduate.

In spite of various and increased attention devoted to the employment problems of handicapped workers, much remains to be done. Research suggests that although school counselors are perceived by students with disabilities to be helpful in general ways, counselor involvement with them is not oriented toward the concrete issues of transition from school to postschool life (Sewall & Humes, 1988).

The high school counselor could be an important force in improving the career/educational placement opportunities for disabled students. Three broad areas serve to define the role of the counselor regarding job replacement:

- Help students obtain employment through systematic efforts to develop interviewing and job seeking skills.
- Help college-bound students select schools and programs most suited to their needs, interests, and abilities.
- Serve as a school liaison with agencies and local employers to encourage the employment of students with disabilities.

Developing Employability Skills

Handicapped workers repeatedly report that the most difficult task related to employment concerns **getting a foot in the door.** Technical or vocational qualifications, good interpersonal skills, and appropriate work habits are of little value unless the student is able to **sell** himself or herself to a prospective employer. The school counselor can help disabled students develop necessary skills and techniques through individual conferences, group guidance sessions, structured course work, or extracurricular activities.

One of the most difficult areas for many students with disabilities to prepare for concerns the job interview. Often, disabled students have little or no idea of the purpose of an interview, much less of what to expect during an interview. Although research has consistently shown the job interview to be an invalid and unreliable predicator of job performance, it continues to be the single most widely used method of employee selection.

Research indicates that interviewing skills can be taught to many populations, including retarded people. Although a variety of approaches such as role playing, didactic instruction, and modeling are available and show promise, the most effective programs appear to be those that have employed a combination of techniques, strategies, and materials.

Helping students prepare for the kinds of questions they will be asked is one of the most important aspects of interview training. Coping with questions concerning the disability can be a problem unless students feel selfassured and able to communicate their confidence.

The counselor's role in the actual job placement of students with disabilities will vary according to factors such as skill and interest of the counselor, availability of community or state placement agencies, and age, interests, and level of job preparation of students.

Helping Students Select a College

In one sense, disabled college-bound students face the same decisions as do nonhandicapped students who wish to continue formal education beyond high school. Factors such as geographical location, enrollment, majors and programs available, extracurricular activities, and cost are considerations that will help determine the most appropriate institution. Many disabled students, however, must also base their decisions on other factors such as architectural accessibility; availability of reader, interpreter, or attendant care services; or access to special equipment and housing.

Accessibility is a prime requisite of a college or vocational center for many physically handicapped students. Although architectural barriers are usually cited as the primary deterrent to college attendance by disabled students, the truth is that such barriers are only one obstacle. Housing, transportation, and financial aid are probably more important and more difficult problems to solve than purely architectural difficulties.

Since oral communication is a fact of life on the typical college campus, deaf students who choose to attend college in the mainstream will need to be able to obtain resources and assistance to facilitate their communication. Interpreters can greatly aid the deaf student in class, as well as during various field assignments. Noninterpreters, such as work-study students, can help by taking notes and asking questions. A variety of mechanical aids and devices can facilitate communication for the deaf student.

The primary obstacles that visually handicapped students encounter in college concern obtaining appropriate reading material and/or services. Readers can help by taping texts and papers, assisting with library research, and reading tests. A training course for readers will help insure their expertise and dependability. Texts can be recorded, reproduced in large print, or presented in braille, according to the needs of individual students. The student will need to contact individual instructors at least two months prior to the start of a course to obtain the title and other information concerning the text.

Blind college students today have access to an increasing number of other aids and devices that can enhance their educational experiences. Braille or talking calculators, speech compressors, and devices that convert printed letters into braille or voiced versions are all commercially available, and constant research is resulting in additional devices and lowered costs.

Spinal cord injured and other orthopedically or neuromuscularly handicapped students may require assistance with mobility and/or personal care while on the college campus. Architectural considerations are particularly important to students who must maneuver through a variety of buildings on crutches or in a wheelchair. Ramps, low controls on elevators, wide doorways, and accessible rest rooms are just a few of the many considerations that physically handicapped students must consider as they select facilities to meet their needs. Fortunately, numerous aids and services are available to help physically handicapped people with mobility and related difficulties.

Attendant care may be required by some severely disabled students. Some colleges have attendant training programs, nurses on dormitory duty, and related services. Others may have no facilities or personnel to cope with common problems such as spasms, pressure ulcers, or related physical concerns.

Communicating with Agencies and Potential Employers

Local, state, and federal agencies are vital to the educational and vocational placement of disabled students. They can and do assist students in obtaining financial aid for college, in determining eligibility for disability payments, and in obtaining technical training and/or employment, among countless other services. Many agencies employ trained counselors who are experienced in working with clients with particular handicapping conditions; these counselors are invaluable referral sources and can often provide the more generally trained school counselor with helpful advice and moral support. It is the responsibility of school counselors to identify local services available for students with disabilities. Examples of agencies that are found in most communities and are actively involved in the career and educational placement of handicapped individuals include the local vocational rehabilitation agency, Goodwill Industries, Lighthouse for the Blind, Jewish Employment and Vocational Service, and the local branch of the state employment service.

The development of collaborative efforts and a solid professional working relationship with community agencies may depend on the care with which personal contacts are made. Likewise, the value that disabled students place on the services provided by these agencies may rest with their reputation among school staff. Counselors can facilitate the development of a working partnership by visiting with each agency and becoming personally acquainted with the roles of various staff members. Once formal liaisons are established, referrals will be easier and direct services to individual students enhanced.

Although numerous agencies may become involved with career and educational planning of disabled students, one in particular merits special mention. The state Vocational Rehabilitation agency is the single most influential and wide-ranging source of vocational assistance for handicapped individuals. Among the services provided by Vocational Rehabilitation are full evaluation of an individual's work capacity, prostheses to increase physical capacity, funds for vocational or prevocational training, interpreter and reader services, and vocational placement and follow-up.

Although policy varies among states, the Vocational Rehabilitation agency usually begins service at age sixteen. Students should be referred several months in advance in order for the agency to establish eligibility and collect needed diagnostic and medical data.

The fact that the majority of disabled individuals remain in their home community following completion of their formal education underscores the need for counselors and other school personnel to develop cooperative working relationships with local employers.

One method that has proven successful in terms of building relationships between the school and the business community and in placing qualified disabled students in jobs is the concept of a community-school day. Employers and other representatives of the business community are invited to spend a day at the school, both for the purpose of explaining the nature of their business and the types of workers they need and to learn more about hiring disabled workers. Part of the program can focus on information. Some employers are misinformed regarding the effect of employing handicapped workers on Workmen's Compensation premiums, accident rates, and related factors. Such information must be presented by individuals who hold a high degree of credibility with employers, preferably a respected business person who has had personal experience in employing handicapped workers.

Beyond information, employers must have an opportunity to be persuaded through personal contact and experience that disabled workers are competent workers. Skits, mock interviews with handicapped students, and simulations in which handicapped students and employers reverse roles can all be used to develop positive attitudes while making the point that **disability must not be confused with inability.**

Career guidance can never be divorced from the mainstream of the educational program. In itself, career guidance encompasses all of the elements of a comprehensive guidance program: counseling, consultation, assessment, planning, and decision-making. For disabled students, the career guidance component of the educational program may be the most vital determinant of their future life-style. Counselors, other guidance personnel, and school staff must work cooperatively in order to design and implement a transitional plan (Rose, Friend, & Farnum, 1988) that will insure that students with disabilities are provided with the best possible chance to succeed in the world of work, and thus in society at large.

Chapter Six

ASSESSMENT OF STUDENTS WITH DISABILITIES

Traditionally, the school counselor's role with the student assessment program has been primarily supportive. In most schools, counselors have served in coordinating and clerical positions with regard to the standardized testing program. Although counselor time devoted to general assessment is often substantial, most group-oriented standardized tests are administered by classroom teachers. The counselor's functions have been generally concerned with such tasks as scheduling testing hours, monitoring large group testing, checking answer sheets for correctness, and collecting test booklets from individual classroom teachers. Individual testing is usually conducted by a school psychologist; in some cases, counselors administer interest or aptitude tests to individual students who seek information about their own skills and abilities. In general, the counselor's assessment functions have been seen and treated as a **necessary evil** and certainly not an integral part of the concept of services to students.

PL 94-142 has insured that assessment is viewed as an important and integral component of the educational experiences of students with disabilities. The mandates of the law regarding assessment are extensive and specific, and they have drastically affected the roles of school counselors.

ASSESSMENT AND PL 94-142

Two general purposes of an assessment program are to assist in the determination of a student's current functioning in a variety of domains and to predict future behavior. Both purposes are important for students with disabilities. The determination of current functioning is an objective mandated by law; it is an integral concept of the Individualized Education Program that proceeds from assessment (see Chapter 1). The prediction of future performance, while not required by law, is recognized as important to career success and social adjustment of students with disabilities.

The requirements of the assessment procedures under PL 94-142 are very specific:

> Testing and evaluation materials and procedures used for the purposes of evaluation and placement of handicapped children must be selected and administered so as not to be racially or culturally discriminatory.
>
> State and local educational agencies shall insure, at a minimum, that:
>
> (a) Tests and other evaluation materials:
>
>   (1) Are provided and administered in the child's native language or other mode of communication, unless it is clearly not feasible to do so;
>
>   (2) Have been validated for the specific purpose for which they are used; and
>
>   (3) Are administered by trained personnel in conformance with the instructions provided by their producer.
>
> (b) Tests and other evaluation materials include those tailored to assess specific areas of educational need and not merely those which are designed to provide a single general intelligence quotient;
>
> (c) Tests are selected and administered so as to best insure that when a test is administered to a child with impaired sensory, manual, or speaking skills, the test results accurately reflect the child's aptitude or achievement level or whatever other factors the test purports to measure, rather than reflecting the child's impaired sensory, manual, or speaking skills (except where those skills are the factors which the test purposes to measure);
>
> (d) No single procedure is used as the sole criterion for determining an appropriate educational program for a child; and
>
> (e) The evaluation is made by a multidisciplinary team or group of persons including at least one teacher or other specialist with knowledge in the area of the suspected disability.
>
> (f) The child is assessed in all areas related to the suspected disability, including, where appropriate, health, vision, hearing, social and emotional status, general intelligence, academic performance, communicative status, and motor abilities. In interpreting evaluation data and in making decisions, each public agency shall draw upon information from a variety of sources, including aptitude and achievement tests, teacher recommendations, physical condition, social or cultural background, and adaptive behavior (Federal Register, August 23, 1977, pp. 42496–42497).

The underlying theme of the legal requirements concerning assessment is that the primary consideration must be the individual child. Decisions must be reached only after careful deliberation, and even then they must be considered tentative.

Implications for Counselors

One of the primary features of the assessment process under PL 94-142 is the fact that it is perceived as an ongoing function. As such, assessment is viewed as a process rather than as a product; it is a means to evaluate, predict, and monitor a student's progress in all domains. Assessment of students with disabilities, then, is an activity that will occur throughout the school year; the counselor's plan for guidance services will need to reflect the continuing involvement.

Assessment of students with disabilities must include both **quantitative** and **qualitative** measures, as opposed to the usual concept of testing as pertaining only to quantitative indices. The emphasis on multifactored assessment presents several implications for counselors. First, it significantly reduces the impact of standardized test results in the decision-making process. Counselors have long protested the heavy emphasis placed on quantitative measures of student performance and have advocated more informal, qualitative, descriptors. While a broadened perspective of assessment meets the approval of most counselors, it will also mean an increased emphasis on qualitative measures requiring specific skills and a considerable degree of subjective judgment. Most counselors have had little experience with systematic classroom observation, structured interviews, or sociometric techniques. These procedures, however, are among those qualitative measures that are used in the assessment of students with disabilities.

The assessment mandate of PL 94-142 implies, and in fact dictates, a team approach. Elementary counselors, in particular, are playing a major role in the assessment process and are often designated coordinators of the assessment team. As coordinator, the counselor will need to demonstrate the ability to work cooperatively with a diverse group including parents, classroom teachers, the school psychologist, the principal, the social worker, and other specialists. The counselor will need to be familiar with the personal and professional strengths of each individual and to be able to facilitate the group's interaction in order to maximize the contributions of each person.

Problems with Tests

In recent years, the use of tests as tools in educational decision making has come under widespread attack. In some parts of the country, moratoriums on testing have been established in an effort to draw attention to various issues and increase efforts to solve some longstanding testing problems. The inadequacies of tests are underscored through litigation based on the unfounded use of IQ scores as the sole criterion for educational placement. As a result, increasing numbers of educators advise the use of standardized tests as only one part of a comprehensive assessment process (Guidubaldi, Perry, and Walker, 1989).

One of the major issues concerning assessment instruments involves the concept of **test bias.** The question of whether or not tests are biased is not a simple issue. Some writers assert that **all** tests are biased to some degree, while others consider that bias is evident only in given circumstances. The most frequently mentioned factors in bias include language, anxiety level, speed and practice conditions, and cultural differences in motivation. However, bias is more complex than is often suggested, and it represents an issue with several facets.

A common contention is that the content of individual items of a test are biased against certain populations. If students have not been exposed to the material covered or if questions are presented in an unfamiliar format, test bias is charged. As an example, item bias against students with hearing impairments has been claimed in several standardized achievement tests because of problems with linguistic structures.

A form of test bias that has proven difficult to research but appears to have particular implications for students with disabilities concerns the effects of **atmosphere** on the testing situation. Although examiners are consistently reminded of the importance of rapport and comfort in the testing situation, some environmental aspects are beyond an individual's control. Testing may be counterproductive with children who must cope with problems of negative attitudes and overt rejection by others. Whereas support and encouragement may be called for, testing procedures may only serve as a painful documentation of the discouragement that some students face.

Another problem with tests concerns different results obtained when norm referenced and criterion referenced measures are used. On **normative referenced tests**, an individual's scores are compared to standard or group scores; often, the comparison is accomplished through derived rather than raw scores and the results reported in grade equivalents, mental ages, stanines, or percentiles. In **criterion referenced testing,** a student's performance is evaluated in terms of an absolute or specific criterion that has been established for that student. The student may be asked to master specific learning objectives or to attain certain skills, without regard for the performance of others.

The vast majority of published tests in both psychology and education are **norm referenced,** although there is increasing emphasis on the importance of criterion referenced instruments, particularly with handicapped students. In terms of designing instructional programs, norm referenced tests have distinct weaknesses. They are unable to pinpoint individual student strengths and weaknesses; they offer little, if any, information concerning appropriate instructional strategies; they cannot predict success beyond the academic situation; and they have limited value for program planning. Further, most norm referenced tests have not included students with disabilities in standardization samples (Fuchs, Fuchs, Benowitz, and Barringer, 1987). However, there are certain limitations and dangers in the sole use of criterion referenced instruments. Too-difficult criteria can lead to failure and frustration, while too-easy criteria can fail to provide challenge. Most counselors and teachers are inexperienced in test construction, a situation that can easily lead to inappropriate criteria.

Other Assessment Problems

Examiner skill and experience are often assumed to be adequate in testing situations, and appropriate procedures of administration, scoring, and interpretation are considered axiomatic. However, in terms of testing students with disabilities, problems with examiner competence are commonplace. Prior to the implementation of PL 94-142, the need for examiners skilled in testing students with various handicaps was not great. Since the passage of the law, demand for skilled examiners has increased far beyond the capacity of training programs to meet needs. The demand for qualified test administrators is made more difficult by two facts: (a) different procedures and skills are often needed with different handicapped populations and (2) in order to assess students with various needs, skill with a wide variety of tests is required.

Another assessment problem concerns the difficulty of using tests for the identification of certain handicaps. For example, **learning disabilities** and **emotional disturbance** are defined broadly, loosely, and with little degree of consensus from state to state. Because of the difficulty of identification, state regulations have been extremely flexible and the programs have not been closely monitored. Unfortunately, this looseness has served to discourage the development of better assessment instruments for use in the identification of these two conditions.

Another pervasive difficulty concerning assessment of students with disabilities is the frequent lack of parental involvement. One of the major reasons why PL 94-142 is explicit concerning parental rights is because those rights have often been violated by educators. The schools have been so paternalistic that a current difficulty is to convince parents that they have both rights and responsibilities concerning their children's education. Involving parents is important, not just from a legal standpoint but also for the process of gathering data. Without knowledge of a student's behavior in the nonschool environment, professionals could mislabel a child for the seeming inability or unwillingness to conform to school standards.

Another problem concerns the implications of modifying test procedures to meet individual needs. While the necessity for certain modifications is often self-evident, little knowledge is available that suggests the resulting effects of such modification on test performance. Research efforts have not been widely undertaken to determine how nonhandicapped students perform with the modifications, nor have studies examined the differential effects with disabled students using varied procedures.

In spite of the fact that assessment provides numerous problems for students with disabilities and raises questions for which there are no easy answers, educators will undoubtedly have to live with the dilemmas. Regardless of the difficulties, assessment procedures are more exact than subjective judgment. Testing, like many other controversial aspects of education, is likely to remain. The responsibility of the counselor is to recognize the vulnerability of assessment and to use it with care. Assessment procedures must be individualized. A variety of qualitative and quantitative measures should be used in order to serve as checks and balances. Interpretation of results must continue as a tentative, cautious process, with a variety of environmental and physical factors considered.

ASSESSMENT OF STUDENT CHARACTERISTICS

Intelligence Testing

The nature of intelligence and its measurement have undoubtedly generated more discussion and controversy than any other topic in psychological and educational literature. Debates continue because of lack of agreement concerning definitions of intelligence, the degree to which intelligence is molded by environmental and hereditary factors, and the role of intelligence testing in educational decision making.

In recent years, the measurement of intelligence has come under widespread attack, and IQ tests have fallen into disfavor. Much of the criticism stems from overdependence and unwarranted use made of intelligence tests in the labeling and educational placement of minority, foreign born, and handicapped students. Litigation and legislation have helped to insure that the use of intelligence measures is kept in proper perspective.

Although much criticism of intelligence tests has focused on the limitations and misuse of the instruments, some objections have been based more on emotional, political, or social arguments.

The advantages of current individual measures of intelligence outweigh their limitations **when the tests are used properly.** However, whenever the instruments are employed for unorthodox purposes, administered by unqualified examiners, or used in unwarranted circumstances, the validity of the instrument becomes suspect.

The Wechsler Scales

The most frequently employed individual tests of intelligence are the Wechsler scales. The three tests: **Wechsler Adult Intelligence Scale-Revised (WAIS-R), Wechsler Intelligence Scale for Children-Revised (WISC-R), and Wechsler Preschool and Primary Scale of Intelligence (WPPSI)** share many common features. For example, each test yields a Verbal IQ, a Performance IQ, and a Full-scale IQ. All items are grouped into subtests of increasing difficulty.

The **WISC-R** is the test most frequently employed in the assessment of school-aged youth, since its age span is 6 through 16 years. The fact that the test yields both verbal and performance (nonverbal) scores has undoubtedly contributed to its popularity with diverse groups, including students with disabilities. Another helpful aspect of the **WISC-R** is that individual subtest scores can be obtained and areas of particular strength or weakness readily observed.

In spite of the fact that the standardization sample of the **WISC-R** did not include identified disabled children, it has proven a popular instrument with students with diverse handicaps. Verbal Scale subtests are often employed as a general measure with visually disabled children, while students with hearing impairments are frequently tested only with the Performance Scale subtests. It is the most frequently employed intelligence measure with learning disabled and mentally handicapped students.

The Stanford-Binet Intelligence Scale

An outgrowth of the work of the French psychologist Alfred Binet, the **Stanford-Binet** is the most well known test of general intelligence in existence and is still in wide use as a global measure. The test has undergone numerous revisions, most recently in 1986 (Thorndike, Hagen, & Sattler, 1986).

The test is organized by years from age 2 to superior adult; between ages 2 and 5, results are scored in half-year intervals, while scoring at age 6 and above occurs at full-year intervals. Unlike the **Wechsler**, which is arranged according to particular subtests, the **Stanford-Binet** contains a variety of items classified only by mental age level. Specific procedures are established for determining a basal age (the starting point) and the ceiling (the stopping point). The **Stanford-Binet** yields a mental age score and an IQ, which is based on a mean of 100 and a standard deviation of 16.

The 1986 version of the **Stanford-Binet** underwent a fairness review to help prevent cultural or ethnic bias. It has been shown to successfully identify mentally handicapped, gifted, and learning disabled children. Nevertheless, it is not useful for severely retarded persons and the reliability of several subtests is quite low (Luftig, 1989, p. 203).

Tests Designed for Students with Disabilities

Most adaptations of intelligence tests have been designed for hearing impaired or visually impaired individuals, although some efforts have been made to modify instruments to accommodate the needs of orthopedically and neuromuscularly disabled people. Several such instruments will be described briefly.

- **The Columbia Mental Maturity Scale** was originally designed as an intelligence measure for children with cerebral palsy, although it has since achieved more widespread use. It requires no verbal response and very little motor responses; it can be administered in 20 minutes. Although it was designed for children aged 3½ through 9, it has been most frequently employed with preschool and early elementary children. Unlike the **Stanford-Binet** and the **WISC-R**, the **Columbia Mental Maturity Scale** can be administered by an individual with a minimum of special instruction.

- **The Peabody Picture Vocabulary Test-Revised,** like the **Columbia Mental Maturity Scale,** is a nonverbal measure that can be quickly administered with a minimum of special preparation.
- **The Haptic Intelligence Scale** was developed for use with blind persons aged 16 to 24 as a performance measure of intelligence. Although it was intended to be used in conjunction with the Verbal Scale of the **WAIS,** the **Haptic** has not been widely employed. Some reasons for its lack of popularity include administration time (2 hours), norms only for functionally blind people aged 16 and over, and the cost. The **Haptic** is, however, a well-constructed performance measure.
- **The Hiskey-Nebraska Test of Learning Aptitude** is a nonverbal test that uses pantomime directions for administration. It has been normed on hearing impaired populations but standardization procedures are weak.

A wide variety of intelligence tests are used in the process of screening and assessing students with disabilities. Some tests such as the **Slosson Intelligence Test** and the **Otis-Lennon Mental Ability Test** can be employed with groups or with individual students and are most often used as brief screening devices. Others, including the **Pictorial Test of Intelligence,** the **Leiter International Performance Scale,** and the **Blind Learning Aptitude Test** have separate norm groups for certain exceptionalities. However, tests developed specifically for a given population may not be as useful as more general instruments because of design problems. In short, the measurement of intelligence is a risky undertaking that can have long-lasting effects on the life of an individual student. Testing in this area should be comprised of several measures and the limitations of each instrument acknowledged.

Achievement Testing

Group tests of academic achievement are routinely administered in most schools, and disabled students who are mainstreamed will usually participate in the testing process. However, when a handicap prevents a student from participating in a group administration or when the student is being evaluated in preparation for IEP development or review, individual tests will be needed. The assessment of general academic achievement is one of the school counselor's primary responsibilities in the evaluation process. Several general and specific achievement tests that are used frequently with handicapped students include the following:

- **The Wide Range Achievement Test-Revised (WRAT-R)** is a popular, easily administered achievement test of reading, spelling, writing, and arithmetic. The test is easily hand scored, and results can be converted into grade equivalents, standard scores, or percentiles. It is designed for preschool children through adults, and it can be administered in approximately 30 minutes.

- **Peabody Individual Achievement Test (PIAT)** has gained wide acceptance in recent years. The **PIAT** measures achievement in mathematics, reading, spelling, and general information. Reading achievement is measured in two subtests, Recognition and Comprehension. Each of the five subtests of the PIAT provides a grade equivalent, a standard score, and a percentile rank. The test is designed for use with ages 5 through adult. Although it is not timed, the usual administration time is 30 to 40 minutes.

- **The Woodcock Reading Mastery Tests-Revised (WRMT-R)** are a criterion referenced battery designed for use in kindergarten through 12th grade. Six areas are assessed—letter naming, word identification, nonsense word attack, word comprehension, passage comprehension, and total. For each area, scores are reported in grade level, percentile rank, age scores, and criterion reading scores. The entire battery requires about 30 minutes to administer.

- **The Key Math Diagnostic Arithmetic Test-Revised** is designed as a comprehensive assessment of mathematical skills. Three major areas with 13 subtests are included—basic concepts (numeration, rational numbers, geometry); operations (addition, subtraction, multiplication, division, and mental computation); and applications (measurement, time and money, estimation, interpreting data, and problem solving). The tests are appropriate for kindergarten through 8th grade; the entire instrument can be administered in 30–50 minutes.

Literally hundreds of academic achievement tests are available that can be used to assess accomplishment in specific areas. Most such tests will be used in isolated situations and with students who have very specific learning deficits. Counselors and teachers will need to examine various instruments and consult test reviews in order to be sure that the most appropriate test is selected.

Measures of Social Competence and Adaptive Behavior

The assessment of adaptive behavior and social skills has taken on new dimensions during recent years. The inclusion of these areas in current definitions of mental retardation and emotional disturbance has spurred test developers to find more systematic and accurate measures. Unfortunately, the measurement of social and emotional competence is hampered by a lack of well-developed instrumentation and techniques.

Behavior Rating Scales

Among the many checklists or rating scales that are used to depict adaptive behavior or social competence are two that are in wide use: **The Vineland Social Maturity Scale** and **The AAMD Adaptive Behavior Scale— Public School Version.**

The Vineland Social Maturity Scale provides a very gross index of social functioning. The instrument consists of 117 items to which a responsible and knowledgeable adult (parent, other relative, teacher) responds in reference to the child. Questions are grouped in six behavioral domains: self-help, self-direction, locomotion, occupation, communication, and social relations. Scores are compared with **normal life age** scores obtained by nonhandicapped individuals in the standardization sample. Scoring is subjective and is dependent upon numerous judgments and interviewing skills.

The AAMD Adaptive Behavior Scale—Public School Version is a behavior rating scale for mentally retarded, emotionally disturbed, and other developmentally disabled persons. Useful for ages 3 to adult, the **Adaptive Behavior Scale** is designed to measure an individual's effectiveness in coping with the social demands of his or her environment.

The test is divided into two parts. **Part 1: Skills and Habits** involves the following behavioral domains: independent functioning, physical development, economic activity, language and development, numbers and time, domestic activity, vocational activity, self-direction, responsibility, and socialization. **Part II: Maladaptive Behavior** includes the following areas: violent and destructive behavior, antisocial behavior, rebellious behavior, untrustworthy behavior, withdrawal, stereotyped behavior and odd mannerisms, inappropriate interpersonal manners, inappropriate vocal habits, unacceptable or eccentric habits, self-abuse behavior, hyperactive tendencies, sexually aberrant behavior, psychological disturbances, and use of medications.

Classroom Observation

Observation of a child's actual performance in a social or learning situation is increasingly recognized as an important determinant of adaptive behavior. Direct observation is often more reliable than the use of social maturity scales because the interview format of such instruments can lead parents or other involved adults to respond as they desire the child to perform rather than as the child actually performs.

Approaches to observation can be classified into **open** and **closed** methods. Open methods involve the recording of all observed behavior in forms such as narrative descriptions and diary accounts. Essentially, the observer records all interactions involving the student, including conversations, nonverbal communication, and direct actions emanating from or directed toward the student. A generalized but descriptive picture of the classroom environment, the relationship of the student to others in the class, and the student's typical responses to various stimuli will emerge after a series of observational accounts have been described. The advantages of open methods of observation are that a rich and descriptive picture of the classroom environment and an individual's reaction to that environment will develop.

While open observation has the value of presenting a global picture of a child's behavior in the classroom, the technique has obvious limitations. Interpretation and judgment regarding the significance of certain behaviors are always open to question. Thus, **closed** systems of observation are required for more accurate determination of specific adaptive behavior.

Frequency recording is one closed method of observing behavior. In this approach, a particular behavior is observed and noted according to the number of occurrences within a given period of time. For example, if the counselor were recording the frequency of acts of self-abuse by a child, observations would be kept for a specified length of time, such as 30 minute periods, over a period of several days.

In time sampling, another closed method, behavior is noted at different points in time, which can be selected randomly or systematically. Inappropriate talking, for example, could be observed through three 5-minute intervals established at specified times of the day.

A combination of open and closed approaches to classroom observation can help determine the extent to which the regular classroom environment represents the best placement for a student. Observational techniques, when properly recorded, can be used as baseline data, as pre and post-measures of behavior change, as determinants of the interactional effects of teacher and student, or as predictors of academic or social success.

ASSESSMENT OF STUDENTS WITH SPECIFIC DISABILITIES

The validity of results of assessment of students with disabilities is based on several important factors. First, the test, inventory, or assessment procedure must be selected as the best available means of obtaining the needed information. Too often, it is automatically assumed that a formal test is the most legitimate measure simply because it **is** a formalized procedure. However, consideration of the needs and characteristics of an individual student may well result in the conclusion that interviews, observational procedures, or an autobiographical essay will provide more accurate and useful information in a given area.

A vital consideration in the assessment of all students is the relationship that is established between the student and the examiner. Counselors sometimes dismiss the notion of **rapport** as a routine technique consisting of asking the student several superficial questions and/or chatting aimlessly about irrelevant topics for a few minutes prior to getting down to the business at hand. Rapport, however, cannot be achieved via a series of steps or adherence to a set of pat phrases. It is a more elusive quality that concerns the manner and attitudes of the examiner more than specific verbalization. But it is important that the student feel as comfortable as possible in the testing situation since fear, uncertainty, and apprehension frequently lead to negatively skewed test scores.

In order to make legitimate comparisons with reference groups, it is important that all instructions regarding the testing situation be followed. The phrasing of directions, time allotted for subtests, scoring procedures, and other aspects of test administration are standard procedures that help validate scores for specific groups.

Interpretation of test results presents a potentially difficult problem with all students. Because the lay public is generally unfamiliar with the limitations of psychometric tests, students and their parents may tend to put more faith in results than is warranted. Part of the counselor's responsibility in the assessment process is to interpret results conservatively and present them judiciously and in an easily understood format.

The regulations promulgated for PL 94-142 specify that the assessment of students with disabilities must be nondiscriminatory. Since few standardized tests have been normed on disabled populations, the validity of a particular test is always open to scrutiny. Additionally, testing procedures must often be adjusted for students with disabilities in order to accommodate physical needs. The skills of the examiner, always a vital component, must extend beyond abilities regarding testing to include knowledge and understanding of a specific handicapping condition. Some guidelines for nondiscriminatory testing of students with disabilities include the following:

- **Test selection and administration must consider potential limitations posed by a disability.** The inability to hear, communicate verbally, see, or manipulate objects may adversely affect test scores or may even prevent a student from completing a particular type of test. A too-high language level on tests of personality, vocational aptitude, or occupational interest may deem such instruments unsuitable for some students.
- **Adaptations in test format and/or administration may be required for many students with disabilities.** For students who must use braille or who have manual difficulties, specified time limits on tests may be unrealistic. Directions may need to be presented orally for blind students or manually for deaf students.
- **The examiner must be thoroughly familiar with the various effects of a student's disability in order to avoid unrealistic expectations regarding performance.** The examiner must be attuned to factors such as fatigue, use of medication, or restrictions in prior social and educational experiences that could affect test performance.

In addition to general testing considerations posed by a disability, students with specific handicaps often have special needs in assessment. The following sections provide brief discussions of the testing process and preferred instrumentation with specific disability groups.

Assessment of Students with Visual Impairment

Research concerning testing with visually impaired people is extremely limited, and most of the information collected has been gleaned through empirical methods. However, as increasing numbers of students with visual impairment are mainstreamed in public schools, counselors are being pressured to participate more actively in assessment functions with them.

Problems in Testing Visually Impaired Students

Testing students with visual impairment presents certain difficulties not necessarily characteristic of other handicapping conditions. The inability to see is, in itself, directly responsible for some difficulties. The measure of some skills, such as mathematical ability, is extremely difficult and involves a different set of skills when computations must be done by memory. For students who must use braille, achievement testing is very time-consuming. Tests themselves present problems whether or not they were normed on visually impaired populations. Standardized measures designed for sighted populations usually present one or more of the following problems:

- If the test is administered orally, the blind person is at a disadvantage by the test requirements, such as having to remember several multiple choice responses while choosing among them.
- Graphs, diagrams, maps, and other graphic material cannot be effectively presented in other forms; achievement tests in areas such as social studies or science are severely restricted by the omission of certain items.
- Most tests contain items in which visualization is a key factor in understanding the concept as well as answering the question.
- Most tests require knowledge which people obtain visually and which it would be unlikely anyone thought of telling a blind child.
- Many tests relate to events which are significantly modified by the fact of blindness, especially activities which cannot be done independently of vision.

Guidelines for Assessment of Visually Impaired Students

Experience has generally proven to be the most effective teacher in familiarizing professionals with facilitative assessment of students with visual impairment. Some guidelines for assessment include the following:

- **The counselor should become informed of the etiology, characteristics, and prognosis of the student's visual handicap.** It is important to be aware of the amount and quality of the student's visual history and the types of learning aids employed.

- **The examiner should meet with the student's parents prior to testing.** In addition to the legal rights of parents to give informed consent for testing, discussion of the child's visual condition and emotional characteristics can provide the counselor with valuable information concerning the student's possible reactions to testing and strategies for putting the child at ease.

- **The student should be treated as an individual rather than as a "blind person."** The examiner should avoid talking in loud tones or making obvious procedural alterations. Physical contact such as taking the student's arm or touching the student on the shoulder can help facilitate communication.

- **The student should be oriented to the room and the testing situation.** If the student's vision is severely restricted, the counselor should offer an arm or, in the case of young children, take the student's hand to lead the way to the examining room. If the student's hand is placed on the back of the chair, he or she can usually be seated without further assistance. Comments concerning the location of furniture, the presence of a tape recorder, and the general arrangement of the room may help the student feel more comfortable.

- **The examiner should verbally provide the student with as much information about the test as a sighted child would receive visually.** It is vital that the student understand what is expected in the way of test responses. Asking questions of the student can determine whether or not tasks are clearly presented.

- **The examiner must ascertain and use the most appropriate method of presenting test items.** Items may be read aloud, presented in braille, or recorded on tape. Many tests are available in large print, and the American Printing House for the Blind provides braille answer sheets. In the case of young children who profess to be able to use print, it is wise to obtain a demonstration.

- **Time limitations should be reconsidered.** There is little justification for adhering to rigid time limits on any type of test when the primary purpose is to estimate current functioning of students with visual impairment. Some examiners suggest that a student should be allowed to complete a task if it appears that he or she is approaching a solution. If it seems that the problem cannot be resolved regardless of time allowed, the task can be terminated at the completion of the regular time limit.

- **Tests should be administered in short sessions.** Fatigue is frequently a problem with visually impaired students since a great deal of concentration is required when attempting to use braille, large type, or oral means of test taking. Short, multiple sessions are far preferable to a single, long session.
- **Lighting requirements must be considered.** Lighting should be bright but without glare. An oblique light source from the side of the better eye is helpful. Extraneous stimuli such as flickering lights or unnecessary noise must be reduced as much as possible.

Assessment of Students with Hearing Impairment

A primary responsibility of the school counselor with hearing impaired students is to assist in the measurement of intelligence, academic achievement, social and emotional development, and career-oriented interests and aptitudes. The degree and nature of the counselor's responsibility will be largely dependent upon his or her experiences in working with hearing impaired students and ability to communicate in the students' preferred mode. More than any other handicapping condition, profound hearing loss dictates the absolute necessity for special training and skills in various communication modes.

Problems in Testing Hearing Impaired Students

Difficulties in testing students with hearing impairment fall into two general areas: problems with tests and problems with test examiners. In terms of tests, the vast majority of standardized instruments have been normed only on hearing subjects.

Many writers consider standardization to be more of a problem with hearing impaired students than with other handicapped children. In terms of environmental and psychological experiences, deaf and hearing children are extremely different. In spite of normal intelligence, hearing impaired high school graduates are likely to possess reading skills at the fourth grade level and mathematical skills at the seventh grade level. The extremely low reading level negatively affects performance on a wide variety of measures, and the typical disparity between reading and computation levels causes difficulty in selecting the appropriate form of a test, particularly in terms of achievement measures.

Another common characteristic of students with hearing impairments that influences their test scores concerns their lack of motivation to compete with others or to perform to their maximum on psychometric measures. Tests that stress speed or require sustained concentration are particularly susceptible to attitudes of diffidence by many students with hearing impairment, again due to atypical cultural and environmental experiences.

In addition to the many problems posed by the tests themselves are concerns related to the skills of test examiners in assessing hearing impaired people. Common sense as well as legal requirements dictate that students be assessed in their preferred mode of communication. Unfortunately, the vast majority of counselors, psychologists, and others involved in psychological assessment of deaf persons are not skilled in any form of manual communication.

Guidelines for Assessment of Hearing Impaired Students

As counselors begin to assess hearing impaired children and youth, they will need to develop strategies that will help insure a positive experience. Practical suggestions for the evaluation of students with hearing impairments include the following:

- **Examiners need to hold attitudes that are conducive to the development of rapport with hearing impaired students.** Specifically, the examiner should be a person with a genuine liking for children, who is not disturbed by deafness, who is not self-conscious in communicating through various modes, who is patient and flexible, and who is more concerned with understanding the child than with rigidly adhering to test procedures.
- **The examiner should make adequate preparations prior to testing the child.** The examiner should become familiar with the child's background and history and become acquainted with the child before testing. The tests should be selected only after careful examination. The testing room should be made comfortable, orderly, and well-lit.
- **The examiner must determine the needs of each student individually while acknowledging some general guidelines.** Ordinarily, a child with a hearing loss of less than 15 decibels can be given the same test as hearing children. If the loss is 75 decibels or more, procedures devised for students who are deaf must be used. For students with a loss between 20 and 70 decibels, testing should be started with a

performance measure and verbal measures added if they appear warranted.

- **When administering the test, the student's preferred communication mode must be used.** Communication procedures should be established beforehand and, in some cases, objective directions prepared in simplified verbal language, signs, and pantomime. The counselor should face the student so that lips and hands are clearly visible. Interpreters should not be used unless absolutely necessary, especially for intelligence or projective measures.
- **Testing procedures must be conducive to the student's maximum performance.** Practice items should be given to ascertain understanding of the testing procedure. The easiest or least involved tests should be given first in order to reduce anxiety. Testing should be done in small blocks of time in order to alleviate the fatigue involved in coping with communication difficulties.
- **The examiner should record test scores only when convinced that they are within an acceptable range of accuracy.** Given that many test results with deaf children are more experimental than definitive, questionable scores should be replaced by explanatory statements.

Assessment of Students with Learning Disabilities

Unlike most handicapping conditions, learning disabilities are most often detected after the child enters school. Because of the effects of the handicap, the identification of a learning disability and procedures for remediation are often revealed by the same measure.

The primary problems involved with the assessment of learning disabled students concerns disagreement among professionals as to useful definitions. Most criteria regarding learning disabilities involve a significant disparity between intelligence and achievement; thus, measures on both dimensions are generally involved in the determination of disability. Another widely accepted criterion for learning disability involves deviation in terms of visual, auditory, or motor perception. Measures of perception are likewise often included in the assessment of children with suspected learning disabilities.

One of the most popular instruments with learning disabled children is the **Illinois Test of Psycholinguistic Abilities**, although a number of other perceptual measures are frequently used, particularly for screening purposes. Among the most frequently employed are the **Detroit Tests** of Learning Aptitude, the Developmental Test of Visual Perception, the Developmental Test of Visual-Motor Integration, and the Auditory Discrimination Test. Many perceptual measures provide diagnostic information that is awkward to translate into clear and useful educational statements. Another common problem of perceptual tests is that they often require extensive training to administer and interpret.

Because of the wide variability of behavior associated with learning disabilities, assessment for diagnosis and treatment must be comprehensive, including informal as well as formal measures. In many cases, observation of the student in the classroom environment and examination of samples of real life behaviors can provide more useful information than is obtained from standardized instruments.

Numerous learning problems can be identified through the use of informal measures and checklists. In addition to the exactness of information provided, informal tests are usually inexpensive, easily constructed, flexible, and rapidly administered. The purpose of informal evaluation is not to label a student but to prepare an instructional program based upon individual needs. In the case of learning disabled children, for whom education is remediation, informal measures are a particularly important part of the assessment process.

Assessment of Students with Other Disabilities

For children and youth with handicaps such as mild mental retardation, orthopedic problems, or some chronic diseases, psychological and educational assessment present relatively few difficulties. In many instances, no modifications in testing procedures are necessary and standard norms can be used with confidence. An overview of the assessment considerations with students of varying disabilities and suggestions for particular situations are briefly described.

Students with Physical Disabilities

Depending upon the nature and extent of their handicap, testing presents widely differing implications for physically disabled children. In some cases, the impairment is relatively minor in terms of social, verbal, and motor skills; in such situations, tests standardized on non-disabled populations can be used without alterations. At the other end of the continuum are students whose disability may significantly affect all three dimensions. Many students with cerebral palsy, for example, may be difficult to assess because of significant involvement of speech and motor abilities. Further, such students may have been exposed to such limited social and environmental conditions that any measure that relies on typical childhood experiences will be invalid. Physically impaired individuals usually encounter developmental experiences later in life than nonhandicapped people, and their rate of cognitive growth may be uneven. Therefore, measures based on chronological age, such as intelligence, cannot be considered equivalent for disabled and nondisabled students. Motor tasks are performed slowly and laboriously by many physically disabled children. Failure on some tests, such as the various performance subtests of the **Wechsler** scales, cannot be interpreted as limited mental ability. Likewise, the validity and reliability of many instruments, including measures of intelligence, are often dependent on normal speech. Thus, standardized test scores may reflect the extent of a child's physical handicap rather than the level of intellectual ability.

A related problem affecting test performance of students with physical disabilities concerns the effects of medication. Many children with cerebral palsy, epilepsy, or other physical disorders are frequently placed on antispasmodic, anxiety-inhibiting, or anticonvulsive drugs. Many such medicines have direct effects on the central nervous system that can, in turn, interfere with testing procedures and results. The counselor must always be alert to the presence of medication when evaluating students with disabilities and consider possible effects of drugs when analyzing test results.

Students with Mental Handicaps

As with learning disabled students, psychometric instruments are used with mentally impaired children both for purposes of identification/placement and for assessment of educational progress. Also like many learning disabled children, students with mental handicaps are difficult to assess on some standardized instruments because of a number of secondary characteristics associated with their disability. Most of these students have low reading and comprehension abilities, short attention and interest spans, difficulty in following directions, and low tolerance for time constraints. While many standardized tests require a reading level of at least sixth grade, mentally handicapped students seldom achieve reading skills above a fourth grade level. Additionally, these students often have had negative experiences with psychological testing;

tests may serve as blatant reminders of their limitations; few of these students, therefore, are eager to perform in testing situations.

The inclusion of measures of adaptive behavior in the identification of students with mental handicaps is widely supported; however, as discussed earlier in this chapter, significant concerns have been expressed regarding the quality of available instrumentation. Counselors and other school personnel must be careful to include informal measures of adaptive behavior, such as interviews and observation, in the assessment of mentally handicapped students.

Chapter Seven

CONSULTING WITH CLASSROOM TEACHERS

Serving as a consultant to classroom teachers has long been viewed as a major responsibility of school counselors. The American School Counselor Association (ASCA) and the Association for Counselor Education and Supervision (ACES) publicly advocated consultation as one of three major services in 1966 (ACES–ASCA, 1966), and articles on the topic began to appear in the professional literature as early as 1957 (Patouillet, 1957).

In spite of the increasing number of professional books and articles devoted to the general topic of the school counselor's consultation role with teachers, a significant gap has remained between what has been advocated and what has been put into practice. One of the primary reasons cited for counselors' lack of involvement in consultation is inadequate training. In one survey (Comas, Cecil, & Cecil, 1987), approximately 100 counseling **experts** were surveyed to determine the training needs of school counselors. From a checklist of 119 potential needs, the respondents ranked consultation with teachers as the second most prevalent need, with 81% of the group indicating consultation to be a critical area of need.

In spite of the need for training and counselors' relative lack of involvement with the consultation function, most published reports have indicated that counselors can be effective consultants to teachers. Bundy and Poppen (1986) reviewed the professional literature to identify research articles in which elementary school counselors provided consulting services. Of the 21 studies identified, 18 (86%) provided outcome data that showed significantly positive effects of consultation by counselors.

THE COUNSELOR-TEACHER RELATIONSHIP

Until the implementation of PL 94-142, the professional relationships between counselors and teachers were often distant and wary. The move toward mainstreaming, however, has effected role changes and created working partnerships where none before existed. Whereas PL 94-142 has altered the responsibilities of school counselors to a significant degree, it has had an even greater impact on classroom teachers. Like counselors, most teachers have had little training or experience with students with disabilities. They are being called upon to work with students who often present serious behavior or learning problems, and they must confer with parents who are frequently angry or discouraged about their child's disability. Teachers are expected to accommodate widely diverse social and personal needs in classroom environments that are generally not conducive to acceptance of differences and change. They have been expected to screen students for various problems, to devise alternative teaching strategies and other interventions for individual students, to participate in numerous lengthy staffings regarding psychological and educational assessment outcomes, to contribute to the development of complicated Individualized Education Programs (IEPs) for students, and to assume primary responsibility for the implementation of the IEPs for most students with disabilities.

Because of their own lack of preparation for the mainstreaming movement, classroom teachers have had to turn to others within the school for assistance. Although special education personnel have been the primary source of help regarding curriculum planning, most other areas of teacher concern have been directed toward counselors. Surveys have shown that teachers desire help from counselors (Hett and Davies, 1985). However, when counselors offer advice and find teachers disregarding it, counselors often become discouraged or angry. Teachers likewise feel defeated and unheard. It is important for counselors to understand that change for classroom teachers, as for anyone, is difficult. Thus, potential changes often evoke resistance and anxiety, regardless of potential benefits. The process of helping teachers work through their own resistance is a challenging one, and represents a task that calls for counselors to be perceived as competent and trustworthy (Margolis & McGettigan, 1988).

Counselors can learn to enhance their consultation skills by understanding and sometimes changing the nature of their relationship with teachers. Since consultation is a process of influence, it involves social power. Counselors often react negatively to the concept of power without understanding its impact upon the consultation process.

There are a number of ways to classify social power, and within the various classifications there are many different types of power. Two forms—expert power and referent power—appear to be particularly applicable to the consultative process (Knapp and Salend, 1984; Martin, 1978).

Expert power refers to the knowledge or skill that is attributed to one person by another. In general, characteristics that are associated with individuals who possess expert power include high levels of education, experience, and maturity. Additionally, expert power is highly restricted in range; that is, expertise is attributed to an individual in a small number of content areas. Following this paradigm, the consultant with the highest degree of expert power will be the person who is older, more highly educated, and who possesses more professional experience than the individuals with whom he or she consults. Further, the successful consultant is likely to have developed a few areas of expertise rather than to have attempted to consult across a broad range of topics.

Although perceived expertise is a necessary characteristic for a consultant, expertise in itself is insufficient. Additionally, the consultant must be viewed as someone with whom the client or consultee can identify. The ability to empathize or create rapport with another individual results in a type of influence that is often called **referent power.** The more similar in values, attitudes, and experiences that a consultant appears to his or her clients, the more they will tend to seek out the consultant's services. Unlike expert power, which is narrowly focused, the person with a high degree of referent power has a significant degree of influence over others in a number of areas.

For the school counselor who seeks to serve as a consultant to teachers, efforts need to be made to develop both expert and referent power. The counselor might begin by performing professional activities that serve to build a reputation in a given area. Selecting an area of expertise, such as guidance of students with disabilities, the counselor can conduct parent groups, contribute to professional journals, make presentations to teacher groups, and conduct other activities that help build a professional reputation. At the same time, the counselor will need to develop compatible and trusting relationships with teachers.

The counselor should carefully select the targets of his or her initial consultation activities. In general, the counselor should attempt to work with the younger, less experienced teachers in a school and defer consulting with the older, more experienced teachers until a reputation is firmly established.

Two broad areas of teacher concern that can be approached through consultant techniques include the following:

- **Teachers need information and assistance in modifying the classroom environment to meet the needs of students with disabilities.** Much assistance concerning teaching strategies is provided by special education teachers and is more in the instructional than in the guidance realm. However, teachers require information related to the personal characteristics and needs of students.
- **Teachers need practical suggestions and help in coping with the stress of teaching, which can lead to teacher burnout.** The incidence of burnout appears to have increased dramatically in the past few years, as evidenced by the number of teachers who leave the profession and those who admit to dissatisfaction with their jobs. Changing societal conditions have affected the classroom atmosphere and contributed to the stress associated with teaching. One of the most influential factors in teacher stress and burnout appears to be the integration of students with disabilities into the regular classroom.

Models of Consultation

Although the functions of helping the teacher control stress, modify materials, and improve classroom environment may all be termed **consultation,** the various procedures followed may differ drastically from one to another. There is no single consultation model that can be molded to fit all classroom issues, nor are there **correct** procedures to follow in any given circumstance. In contrast, a wide variety of models and consultation processes have been identified and discussed in the literature. The selection of a given model may be determined by the theoretical and philosophical orientation of the counselor/consultant, the nature of the presenting problem, or various diverse factors such as who initiates contact, whether consultation is conducted individually or with a group, and the personal relationship between the counselor/consultant and the teacher.

Models or approaches to consultation have been classified in a variety of ways according to differing criteria. Caplan (1970) discussed different approaches in terms of the focus of consultation. In **client-centered consultation,** the focus is on changing the behavior of a student in the classroom by working through the teacher. In **consultee-centered con-**

sultation, the focus is on the concerns of the teacher (consultee) rather than on the student (client).

Process consultation, according to Schein (1978), is based on the assumption that in many situations, the only workable solution must involve the consultee in both the diagnosis and the solution of a problem. Thus, the focus of the consulting effort shifts from the **content** of a given problem to the **process** by which problems are solved. **Process consultation** is designed to increase the problemsolving skills of the client so that future difficulties may be resolved without outside assistance.

Similar to the **process consultation** model is one identified by Kurpius (1978) as **collaboration.** The role of the consultant is primarily one of helping others develop a plan for problem solving; as such, the consultant serves more as a generalist than as a content expert. Like the process consultation approach, the **collaboration** model is based on the assumption that the consultee (teacher) can assume primary responsibility for problem solving in the classroom once he or she becomes attuned to the environmental and interpersonal conditions that facilitate behavior change.

Another model identified by Kurpius (1978) is referred to as **mediation.** Unlike most situations in which the consultee (teacher) would initiate contact, the mediation model is employed when the consultant recognizes a problem, gathers relevant data, and decides upon the most appropriate course of action. At this point, individuals who have the greatest potential to influence change are contacted and requested to intervene. In the school environment, the mediation approach might be employed when the counselor identifies a child or group of children experiencing a particular problem in the classroom. For example, the counselor may become aware of several children with disabilities who are the focus of extremely negative peer attitudes and behavior. The counselor may choose to contact the teacher, explain the situation, and request that the teacher initiate corrective action. The mediation model is not often used other than by highly experienced and reputable consultants. It is, generally, a high-risk approach. It places the consultant in a role uncommon to the educational system and assumes that any individual can be a consultant, regardless of lines of authority.

The counselor's work with classroom teachers appears to mandate the use of at least two approaches to consultation. Some consultative activities may call for a process-oriented approach in which the focus is on general problem-solving ability or communication skills. For example, in helping teachers develop empathy for their students, the counselor serves primarily as a trainer to teachers. In this training role, the focus is on the development of communication and counseling skills that can be implemented by the teacher in the classroom. Likewise, as the counselor consults with the teacher regarding classroom management or remediation of specific behavior problems, a significant aspect of consultation will focus on general teacher-student interaction and communication skills.

Classroom management problems may often relate to specific behavior problems exhibited by particular students. In such situations, the counselor may choose to follow a model in which the student rather than the teacher is considered to **own** the problem. The counselor/consultant provides the teacher with sequential procedures based on specific learning principles for remediation of the problem behavior.

In the counselor's consultative work concerning classroom modifications for students with disabilities, the primary service is the provision of information. Essentially, the teacher requests information on a particular topic such as preparing the classroom to accommodate a student who is physically disabled. The counselor responds by providing the needed information or securing resource materials or people who can assist the teacher. Even in such a cognitively oriented service as providing information, teachers respond much more positively when they are collaborating in the process rather than merely being receivers (Glatthorn, 1990; Myles and Simpson, 1989).

As the counselor works with teachers regarding stress management, several consultative approaches may come into play. The counselor may be primarily involved in providing the teacher with information concerning recognition of symptoms and prevention of burnout. In some cases, the counselors will provide direct training to teachers in order to help them develop more effective strategies to combat stress in their personal lives. In such instances, consultation will focus on both content and process.

The Consultation Process

The particular processes that are implemented during consultation will vary according to the model followed and the nature of the consultative activity. There are, however, some general guidelines concerning consultation that encompass most models and situations.

An obvious difficulty in describing the process of consultation relates to the fact that it is multifaceted, with at least as many variations as would be found in the process of counseling. Generally speaking, individuals who subscribe to a behavioristic view of human nature would demonstrate those ideas not only in their counseling but also in their consultation. Procedures followed would tend to be specific and sequential. They would focus on early clarification of the problem and would include concrete steps of shaping, modeling, or positive reinforcement to obtain the desired behavior. Used in its strictest sense, the consultation process would tend to be highly behavioristic in nature, with the counselor/consultant serving as a teacher and/or model.

Individuals with a cognitive orientation would tend to proceed in consultation much in line with their view of human behavior. Thus a consultant from the cognitive school might consider that teachers' problems in the classroom stem from irrational thought processes that prevent them from using their skills and knowledge in a particular circumstance. The focus of consultation would be on training teachers to view problems from a more objective perspective.

Neophyte consultants often assume that the sole or primary aspect of consultation involves the segment in which the consultant is actively engaged in teaching, modeling, or advising the teacher concerning a plan for change. Overemphasis on this aspect or the relative neglect of the various other components is often responsible for the failure of consultation. The teacher is seldom likely to respond positively to the consultant's suggestions for change unless the teacher feels a considerable investment in and commitment to the process of problem identification, selection of possible solutions, and establishment of objectives. Likewise, neither the currently involved teacher(s) nor future potential consultees are likely to seek consultative services unless evaluation reveals that the consultation plan worked.

In recent years, experts in consultation have begun to stress the importance of personal characteristics in the consultation process. According to Glatthorn (1990), most consultation fails because it over-emphasizes problem-solving and neglects the importance of the consultant-client relationship. West and Cannon (1988) assert that the focus of consultation with teachers should be on interpersonal communication, collaborative problem-solving, and personal characteristics which develop trust and empathy.

Identifying the Problem

Regardless of whether or not consultation is initiated by the teacher or the counselor, the first procedure is to develop a consensus regarding the exact nature of the problem and/or the needs of the teacher. If the situation involves student behavior, the counselor may need to observe in the classroom and interview students and/or parents. Data gathered by the most sophisticated procedures can nevertheless lead to misinterpretation; therefore, the counselor must remain open-minded and cautious concerning the presenting problem until it has been fully explored and discussed. If more than one problem area is defined, the counselor and teacher must collaborate on determining the priority of needs. When several teachers are involved, all should participate in the process of defining the problem area(s) and prioritizing needs. It is often helpful to state the major problem as a need or a goal and to put it in writing for a final perception check by both. Regardless of the procedures used, it is vital to remember than most issues are perceived differently by the various individuals involved, and the process of problem definition is rarely simple (Osterweil, 1987).

Stating Objectives

Once the problem or need is clearly understood and agreed upon by both the counselor/consultant and the teacher, the next procedure is to jointly determine what the ultimate outcome of consultation should be. The solution may involve improved classroom performance or behavior by a given student or group of students; it may concern determination of specific ways to accommodate a handicapped child; it might involve increasing positive communication between teacher and students; or it could concern the determination of methods to reduce stress among all teachers in the school. The objectives should reflect the outcome of the joint efforts between counselor and teachers and should be stated in measurable and observable terms. In order to avoid miscommunication, it is advisable to put the final statement of objectives in writing and include relevant details such as the method that will be used to determine if the problem has been solved, the procedures each person will engage in to solve the problem, the necessary resources, and an appropriate time line.

There is a great tendency of both consultant and consultee to treat the establishment of objectives superficially in a rush to implement the plan.

However, the careful stating of objectives serves several vital purposes and should not be neglected. The interaction that occurs between the counselor/consultant and the teacher during the process of stating objectives is an integral aspect of the consultation process. The statement of objectives should serve as a **work map** or guide to the ensuing activities of the consulting process. It can help keep focus on the topic of concern as well as serve as a reminder of different tasks to be performed.

Implementing the Plan

The plan is developed as part of the statement of objectives. Once it is clearly delineated in as much detail as desired by everyone involved, the action phase of the consultation service can begin. Implementation can involve a myriad of activities, several of which are discussed separately in succeeding sections of this chapter. Regardless of the implementation procedures employed, it will be important for the counselor/consultant and the teacher(s) to periodically monitor progress. The purpose of monitoring, or process evaluation as it is sometimes called, is to determine whether or not everyone involved is proceeding as agreed and that actions are being taken according to the established time frame. Difficulties can be corrected more easily if changes are made soon after problems are discovered. The frequency of meetings for monitoring purposes will depend upon the complexity of the problem to be solved. If the counselor is working with one or two teachers on modifying the classroom environment, the consultation process itself may generally consist of providing information. Thus, monitoring may be a relatively informal process in which the counselor stops by the classroom once a week to check on progress. However, if the consultation plan involves a restructuring of the teacher's methods and style of interacting with students or a systematic means to increase on-task behavior of a particular group of students, monitoring will need to be more formal. In instances such as these, the counselor will need to observe the teacher's practice of new skills and meet frequently to exchange thoughts and give feedback.

Evaluating the Plan

Although the monitoring process is a form of evaluation, it is also considered a part of the actual implementation procedures of a given plan. Monitoring helps both the counselor/consultant and the teacher remain on task, but it does not address the issue of effectiveness. Ultimately, the criterion for successful consultation must involve more than a determination of whether or not everyone followed procedures, completed their responsibilities, or valued the experience. The final questions to be answered must be "Were the objectives accomplished?" and "Was consultation effective in producing the desired change?" The actual procedures to be used in the evaluation process are determined when objectives are developed, so that at this point those procedures would need to be implemented. In most cases, evaluation need not be complex or time-consuming. Overt changes in student or teacher behavior can usually be charted through brief observation and recording methods. As in other phases of the consultation process, it is important that the counselor and teacher work together in evaluating results. The concept of a partnership serves to reinforce the teacher's role in consultation, addresses the importance of each step, and can help build the counselor's credibility among the faculty.

MODIFYING THE CLASSROOM ENVIRONMENT

More often than not, the integration of students with disabilities into the regular classroom can be accomplished with relative ease from an instructional standpoint. Since one of the primary purposes of mainstreaming is to allow special students to experience the same environmental conditions as their non-handicapped peers, drastic reorganization of the classroom is unwarranted. However, there are instances in which certain modifications are mandatory if the students are to be able to participate in the majority of classroom activities. Regular classroom teachers frequently express anxiety concerning mainstreaming efforts because they feel unprepared to alter the classroom to meet special needs.

School counselors are often called upon to help teachers prepare the classroom to receive students with disabilities by providing the teacher with very general information concerning students and their individual needs or by obtaining books and other materials in a given content area.

General Modifications

In order that plans can be made for a student with a disability, the teacher needs to have complete information concerning the nature and extent of the disability, areas of particular strength and weakness, special difficulties and needs in communication and mobility, and any other characteristics that would be manifested in the classroom. If possible, the teacher should plan to meet with the student prior to enrollment in the class. Through this meeting, the teacher can begin to establish rapport with the student, help allay fears or anxieties that the student might be experiencing, and learn firsthand of any particular needs that would require classroom adjustment. Prior to enrollment, the teacher may choose to conduct several classroom sessions designed to prepare the other students for the newcomer. If the child uses various aids or devices such as braces, a wheelchair, or a hearing aid, it may be important to discuss the equipment with other students in order to positively channel their normal curiosity.

In addition to making adequate preparations for a student with a disability, the teacher may wish to use the following general guidelines:

- **Be aware of fatigue.** Many students with disabilities may become tired more easily than other students, and teachers should take steps to prevent and/or to cope with the problem. Fatigue should not be interpreted as disinterest or boredom. It is usually caused by the strain of using several senses or modalities to compensate for a loss.
- **Grade the student on the same basis as other students.** This statement may need to be altered in some instances, particularly students with mental handicaps who may require a totally different set of learning tasks than the majority of students. However, it is important that the student be treated foremost as an able individual and only incidentally as a person with a handicap. When students are graded differently, they view themselves as different, and they are treated differently by their peers.
- **Develop a buddy system.** Many students with disabilities, particularly those with visual, hearing, or orthopedic impairments, can profit from a peer helper at school. The peer might take notes, help the student become oriented to the school, or help the student study. The **buddy** should be a temporary arrangement to avoid the development of overdependence by the disabled student.

Modifications for Specific Conditions

Individual variations are extremely wide, and all classroom modifications must be tailored to specific students. Nevertheless, in very general terms, particular areas of modification can be identified with different handicapping conditions.

Students with Orthopedic Handicaps

The most common classroom modifications required by orthopedically impaired students will concern the physical arrangement of the classroom and the availability of certain equipment. Many orthopedically handicapped students will wear braces or use wheelchairs or crutches. The teacher should become familiar with these appliances in order to provide assistance when needed and help ascertain that the equipment is in good working order.

Students who wear braces are purposely limited in their physical activity. Because most braces are heavy and often prevent flexibility of the spine, students may be slow and clumsy. However, there is no need to further restrict movement. In general, students in braces should be allowed to participate in all physical activities that they are willing to attempt.

Students who use crutches should be seated to the side of the classroom, close to a table. When the student is seated, the crutches should be laid on the floor, under the table. Crutches should never be taken from the child and stored in a remote place.

Students who use wheelchairs must have adequate space to maneuver. Tables and desks should allow the wheelchair to fit underneath, although some students may prefer to use a lapboard.

Some general guidelines for modifying the classroom for physically handicapped students include the following:

- Adjustable tables and chairs are more flexible and useful than immovable seating equipment.
- Overhead projectors are useful since the projected image is usually larger and more easily read than the image that would be visible on a chalkboard.
- A videotape closed circuit television with a large screen allows for easy viewing throughout the room and provides a means for repeated projection of the same information.
- A duplicate set of textbooks and other supplies will eliminate the difficulty some students with physical disabilities have in carrying materials between home and school.

- Classmates can eliminate note-taking problems by making carbon copies of class notes.
- Help should be provided only in situations in which it appears to be needed. The teacher should encourage independence by expecting the same academic performance as that required for other students.

Students with Learning or Behavioral Problems

Students with learning disabilities, mild retardation, or emotional difficulties often share common problems in the classroom. Difficulties with motor coordination, low tolerance for frustration, poor self-concept, short attention span, and below average ability to generalize and conceptualize are characteristics that manifest themselves in the classroom and interact to affect academic performance. The most effective classroom modifications to combat these difficulties appear to concern the teaching strategies employed and the teacher's general approach to communication. As has been stressed throughout this book, poor self-concept is invariably related to poor classroom performance, and self-concept improves only when a degree of personal success is achieved. Therefore, the primary teaching objective must always remain focused on ways to provide opportunities for success and personal mastery.

Aside from the crucial importance of communication style, some instructional procedures are generally more effective than others in combatting problems related to hyperactivity, poor motor coordination, and brief attention span. Motor development, for example, can be approached through direct practice. Games which promote hand-eye coordination are doubly useful in that improved physical performance often results in a more positive self-concept. Concrete applications of learning tasks are generally more effective than abstract approaches with students who experience academic problems. Likewise, assignments should be short in order to maintain interest. Materials such as games and simulations are usually more motivating than traditional teaching approaches and are particularly effective with students who have difficulty with the academic curriculum.

Students with Hearing Impairment

Because most congenitally deaf persons require specialized training not usually available in regular classrooms, most mainstreamed students with hearing impairment will have some degree of hearing. Nevertheless, hearing impaired students in the regular classroom represent a heterogenous population, and their educational needs are extremely diverse. The types of assistance that these students need generally involve ways to facilitate communication.

Since most students with hearing impairment will engage in speech reading to some extent, the teacher and other students should provide conditions that enhance the student's ability to see words formed. When talking to a student with hearing problems, the teacher should face the student directly, at a distance of no more than four feet. Whenever possible, light should be directed onto the speaker's face. Speech should be natural, simple, and clearly enunciated. Shouting or speaking very slowly merely distorts mouth movements and makes speech reading more difficult. If the student appears to have difficulty understanding, clarification can be made by rephrasing or by writing. The teacher must be careful to avoid lecturing while writing on the blackboard, walking around the room, turning the back to the student, covering the mouth while talking, or verbalizing instructions while demonstrating equipment.

Because speech reading has distinct limitations even for those who are proficient in its use, other means must usually be found to augment communication in the classroom. Hearing classmates can provide note-taking assistance by making carbon copies. Interpreters may be used in some circumstances; it is helpful if the interpreter and the teacher can meet prior to the class sessions in order that plans can be made to fingerspell technical words or unusual expressions.

Additional suggestions to make the classroom environment more conducive for learning by hearing impaired students include the following:

- Hearing aids amplify all sounds, not just speech. Noise levels should be kept to a minimum in order to maximize the value of a hearing aid. Windows and doors should be closed when necessary in order to avoid auditory distractions.
- Visual aids such as charts, overhead transparencies, and captioned films can add a useful dimension to learning, provide variety, and reinforce basic concepts.
- Instructional materials must be presented at appropriate reading levels in order to be useful. Classroom discussions and lectures may need to be presented at a vocabulary level that is lower than for most students.
- Hearing aids can often be repaired through a simple change of a battery or a cord. The teacher should collaborate with the student

and/or parents regarding responsibilities for hearing aid repair. For young children, the teacher should learn to do minor repairs in order to avoid the possibility of a wasted day.

Students with Visual Impairment

Students who are blind or partially sighted require more classroom modification than most children since so much academic instruction is visually oriented. Depending upon the degree of useful vision available to the student, alterations may need to be made in the physical arrangements of the classroom, in materials and equipment, and in teaching strategies.

In terms of physical arrangements, conditions should be made such that the student's existing vision is enhanced. Generally, the student should sit toward the front of the room, although the student is the best judge of the most appropriate placement. Students who are visually handicapped should not be seated facing windows nor should they use highly polished desks or tables. Lighting should be modified as necessary to reduce glare.

Equipment and materials for people with visual impairment are extensive; those most useful to the student in a regular class will depend on the student's primary mode of written communication and on the degree of useful vision. Functionally blind students who use braille will require different types of materials and aids than students who can use print for reading. Fortunately, a wide variety of learning materials is available in braille, on audio cassettes, and in large print. In many cases, **all** students can benefit from teaching materials that were designed for people with visual impairment. Records and tapes, for example, encourage the development of auditory learning modes and can provide a welcome change in teaching approaches. Visually impaired students can generally tape-record lectures for study purposes; however, note-taking procedures using a braille stylus are also helpful to blind students.

Although most students with visual impairment can benefit from traditional teaching methods of lecture and discussion, they may require additional learning through the use of different types of equipment. Braille maps, rulers, and typewriters are among the many pieces of equipment that can facilitate classroom learning.

In terms of teaching strategies, a **hands-on** approach is particularly important with students who are visually impaired since they may have difficulty grasping some concepts in spite of a well-developed ability to discuss them. Instruction should always begin at a concrete level and should include, whenever possible, tactile means of expressing concepts and ideas. In order to help the student feel less isolated, the teacher should use the student's name when speaking to him or her and remain in close physical contact.

COMBATTING TEACHER BURNOUT

In the past several years, literature has made frequent reference to the **burnout** phenomenon and its impact on educators. Job burnout has been defined as a psychological process—a series of attitudinal and emotional reactions—that an employee experiences as a result of job-related and personal experiences (Schwab, Jackson, and Schuler, 1986).

Professionals who work in situations involving close personal contact and emotional involvement with others are particularly susceptible to job stress and thus to burnout. A key element in various factors that cause stress appears to be **responsibility for others.** Thus, persons whose occupations most directly involve responsibility for the safety, welfare, or health of others experience considerably more stress-related disease than do persons whose jobs are not so intimately concerned with others' well-being. A dramatic laboratory experiment (Kahn, 1978) vividly illustrates the stress associated with responsibility for others. Pairs of monkeys were situated so that they were inaccessible yet visible to each other. An electric shock was administered to the pairs at regularly scheduled intervals. One monkey had access to a lever which, if operated in time, prevented the shock to both monkeys. Thus, both monkeys in each pair received the same number of shocks at the same time, although only one in each pair was able to control the number of shocks delivered. Over a period of 48 days, **all** of the monkeys with access to the lever died of gastrointestinal lesions. None of the partner monkeys died, nor did any of them develop gastrointestinal problems.

Causes of Teacher Stress

Although counselors are definitely susceptible to job stress and the problem of counselor burnout appears to be increasing, the phenomenon is even more prevalent among teachers. A number of factors have been identified as contributing to the stress of teachers, including increasing school violence and vandalism, disruptive students, involuntary transfers, and oversized classes. A number of studies (e.g. Brissie, Hoover-Dempsey, & Bassler, 1988; Hock, 1988; Wyly & Frusher, 1990) have indicated that the primary sources of burnout are related to organizational conditions (role conflict or ambiguity, lack of autonomy, absence of administrative and peer support, lack of rewards). Personal factors (age, expectations for students, expectations for one's career goals) are also related to burnout (Anderson & Iwanicki, 1984; Bhagat & Allie, 1989; Mazur & Lynch, 1989).

Since the implementation of PL 94-142, increasing attention has been paid to the phenomenon of stress and burnout of teachers of handicapped students. Although teachers at both elementary and secondary levels have expressed commitment to mainstreaming for most students with disabilities, the implementation of the concept has posed considerable problems for the classroom teacher. Teachers often have had no input into the design of mainstreaming programs, in spite of the fact that they hold the major responsibility for their success. Anxiety concerning teaching methods, classroom modifications, and other changes made necessary by the presence of students with disabilities have been misinterpreted by critics who assert that teachers have neither the patience nor the desire to teach handicapped students (Bakewell, 1988; Hohn, 1985).

General causes of stress for classroom teachers, some of which have been directly attributed to the mainstreaming movement, include the following:

- **Work overload and time pressures** brought about as a result of the need for involvement in IEP meetings, parent conferences, and related additional functions.
- **Lack of perceived success** with some children, regardless of efforts expended. How the teacher perceives the situation rather than the reality of it determines the teacher's response and contributes to lowered self-esteem and self-confidence.
- **Specific activities involved with PL 94-142,** particularly diagnosis and assessment. Other new tasks for which teachers feel unprepared also create stress.
- **Isolation from colleagues and alienation from the professional environment.** Teachers have little opportunity to interact with their peers and to give or receive emotional support. Lack of participation in school decision making is a primary contributor to low teacher morale.

- **High ratios of students to teachers.** In general, the more students a teacher is responsible for, the more that classroom problems and opportunities for stress are created.
- **Role conflict created by the demands of a diverse student population and various administrative requirements.** Teachers of children with disabilities are often caught between the need to provide special attention to those students and the need to attend to the demands of the majority of their students. Administrative requirements associated with PL 94-142, parental demands, and various legislative and state requirements for accountability and the teaching of certain skills cause inevitable conflicts in role.

One of the debilitating and dangerous aspects of teacher burnout is the fact that its influence extends beyond the teacher to the students in the classroom, to other staff members in the school, and to the teacher's own family. Continued emotional stress usually results in the teacher's withdrawal from personal contact with others, particularly students.

The teacher may begin by reducing eye contact with students and proceed with other distancing techniques until he or she reaches a point where little positive verbal or nonverbal communication with students remains and the teacher has become indifferent to their needs. Or, teachers may respond by imposing unnecessary authoritarianism on the students, overreacting to minor incidents, and imposing excessive punishment. Concurrently, the teacher may begin avoiding contact with colleagues, eating alone, leaving school early or arriving late, or missing faculty meetings. When teachers **do** interact with colleagues, they may engage in certain behaviors that illustrate a pattern of dehumanization. For example, burned-out teachers may refer to students in derogatory terms. They may become excessively cynical, stubborn, and inflexible, refusing to acknowledge the value of or to participate in any form of change.

Little information is available that indicates the extent to which teachers seek counseling or other forms of personal assistance to combat stress. Although mutual support is recognized as one of the principal means of both prevention and remediation of occupational burnout, there are few indications that such support is made available to teachers. In most cases, teachers are reluctant to discuss their stress because of misguided feelings of guilt, and they seldom realize that the phenomenon is widespread.

The school counselor can provide support services to teachers in the prevention and treatment of stress and burnout through two major activities. First, the counselor can provide teachers with basic information on stress in order that the teachers can learn to recognize symptoms in themselves and to realize that the condition is not unique or indicative of maladjustment. Additionally, the counselor can help teachers provide support for each other and assist them in devising ways to combat stress permanently and positively through in-service workshops and discussion groups.

Information Concerning Stress Reduction

The value of information is too frequently overlooked among guidance strategies. Often, however, information is the major need of a consultee or client. In the case of consultative work with teachers concerning stress and burnout, the counselor's job often consists of informing teachers, individually or collectively, of specific techniques to prevent or reduce stress. Suggestions for the **prevention** of emotional stress and resultant burnout of teachers of students with disabilities include the following:

- The teacher should learn as much as possible about the needs and characteristics of students with disabilities **prior** to their entering the regular classroom. If a program can be designed in advance and necessary classroom modifications made, the teacher's anxiety will be reduced.
- The teacher should arrange for regular opportunities to share classroom experiences and concerns with other teachers and the counselor. Emotional support is essential for the prevention of burnout.
- The teacher should arrange the teaching schedule so that periods of direct contact with students are not prolonged. Team teaching, the use of learning centers, and individual projects allow teachers to withdraw periodically from direct contact.
- Physical exercise is an excellent means of dispelling accumulated stress. The types of exercise available are limited by the resources and time available at the school, but many teachers have found that 15 minutes of vigorous activity serves as a stress reducer.
- The teacher should recognize the dangers of becoming overly involved with individual students or with school activities. The teacher who spends evenings and weekends working with individ-

ual students or with student clubs after a full week of teaching is in
danger of burning out rapidly.

- Development of productive hobbies or involvement in community
activities that are generally unrelated to the teacher's job is a helpful and healthful stress preventative. Such activities provide feelings of satisfaction and contribution that increase self-esteem and
help dispel frustration.
- Teachers are most effective when they establish realistic goals for
themselves. It is helpful to recognize that the drive for perfection
and competition so common in people who experience great emotional stress is derived from within and can, therefore, be internally
controlled.

In-Service Training to Combat Stress and Burnout

As the problem of teacher burnout becomes increasingly recognized,
in-service training programs may be viewed as a remediative device.
The school counselor can provide effective services to teachers through
developing and implementing workshop-type programs specifically
designed to prevent or combat stress.

Although in-service training of teachers should be preceded by a
needs assessment to determine the precise focus of training, some guidelines for the design and implementation of stress workshops are generally appropriate:

- **Involve the teachers in the design of the workshop.** Obtain and use
suggestions for the general focus of training, including topics such
as the amount of time allotted to small and large group activities
and the availability of "handouts" and other materials.
- **Schedule the workshop at a time preferred by teachers.** Administrators
and in-service coordinators too often schedule training sessions
according to **their** needs rather than following teacher suggestions.
Teachers seldom choose to schedule in-service training at the end of
a workday, although that is when most workshops are held.
- **Keep the workshop brief.** The counselor must plan for enough time
to involve teachers and achieve identified objectives, yet avoid
competing with other activities or causing fatigue. Three hours is
usually sufficient for an introductory session.
- **Vary the modes of presentation within the workshop.** People respond

most positively to training that incorporates a variety of approaches to learning, including lecture, films, demonstrations, and participatory activities. Such a variety helps maintain interest, provides for individual variation in preferred learning styles, and reduces mental fatigue.

- **Include ample opportunity for interpersonal sharing within the time frame.** Most people value the opportunity to interact with colleagues above other aspects of training, and in a workshop on stress management the development of a support system is crucial.

An added benefit of successful counselor-led workshops for teachers is that they provide an excellent means of building credibility and demonstrating facilitative communication techniques. An effective follow-up to a workshop is an on-going support group for teachers, which can be facilitated by the counselor (Boytim and Dickel, 1988). The counselor/consultant who effectively meets teachers' **personal** needs will be sought as a resource to aid the teacher in more effective ways of working with students.

Regardless of the nature of the consultative activity, the counselor needs to move slowly and carefully in the process of helping teachers change. The counselor must first establish a positive relationship with the principal and other school administrators. Their respect will contribute toward the counselor's reputation as a consultant.

The counselor must build credibility among the faculty. Respect and liking cannot be achieved instantaneously and may require a year or more of systematic efforts to demonstrate areas of expertise. An effective way to illustrate certain communication or behavior management techniques is to take over classes on a periodic basis, thus providing both classroom guidance activities for the students and a demonstration of specific leadership skills for the teacher.

The counselor should consult first with teachers who have exhibited confidence in the counselor's skills. Success breeds success, and if the counselor is careful to engage only in those consultation approaches with which he or she is competent, a positive reputation will develop and be transmitted throughout the school.

Finally, counselors should be aware that consulting with teachers may not be an activity that is conducted on a daily basis; however, regardless of the frequency of the activity, it is one that will have far-reaching impact on the role of the counselor in the school.

Chapter Eight

WORKING WITH PARENTS

In recent years, increased emphasis has been placed on the importance of the counselor's work with children's families. It is widely known and accepted that the family represents the single most important influence on the development of the child, and most guidance texts published during the past 10 years devote considerable attention to various theories and techniques related to family consultation and counseling. In actual practice, however, parental involvement in the school guidance program has not approached the level advocated in the literature. Counselors and teachers frequently complain that parents appear to become increasingly less concerned about their children's educational experiences as the students progress through school. Parents often counter that school personnel discourage their involvement. The lack of communication between school and home has often been cited as one of the primary causes of declining test scores, increased discipline problems, and student apathy toward education.

The communication difficulties that are characteristic of parents and school personnel regarding average children have been even more pronounced in terms of students with disabilities. While it is undoubtedly true that some parents have chosen to relinquish responsibility for their disabled children's social and educational development, evidence points more strongly to educational personnel as the primary opponents of parental involvement. Numerous books and professional articles in special education have specifically warned parents against any involvement with their child's academic program, advised teachers to limit contact with parents to periodic reporting conferences, or suggested that the only meaningful parental involvement occurs through professional counseling and psychotherapy.

In recent years, attitudes of both parents and professionals regarding parental involvement with the school have begun to change. For the most part, parents themselves have spearheaded efforts to insure their involvement, and professionals have begun to respond. The formation of activist parent organizations has led to political and social pressures on local, state, and national levels to insure that appropriate services and facilities were made available. As discussed in Chapter 1, federal and state laws now mandate parental involvement in every aspect of the education of children with disabilities. Professional educators have begun to acknowledge a growing body of research that points to the value of parental involvement in educational programs. Numerous studies indicate that working with parents can be more effective in correcting children's behavioral problems than direct intervention with the children themselves (Leyser, 1988).

Parental involvement with the education of children with disabilities is justified on more than legal grounds and research evidence. Parents *know* their children far more completely than can any professional. They understand the child's problems, needs, habits, and patterns of behavior. They are aware of the ways in which the child copes with the disability, and they frequently have a great deal of information about the nature and effects of their child's specific handicap. Neither can any professional *care* about the child in the same way or to the same degree that most parents do. Whereas professionals must necessarily divide their time and attention among a number of children in addition to their personal responsibilities and interests, parents can often devote concentrated efforts to the education and development of a single child. Finally, parental involvement with the education of their handicapped children is justified on the basis of responsibility. No matter how comprehensive, sophisticated, or detailed is the educational and/or remedial program designed for the handicapped child, the parents are ultimately and continuously responsible for decisions affecting that child. As such, they have a need and a right to be working partners with professionals concerning every aspect of their child's education and treatment.

It is important for counselors to remember that parents of children with disabilities are, first of all, individuals. As such, they share basic needs, hopes, and desires with the rest of humanity. At the same time, they possess highly individualized characteristics as do all people. Second, like other parents, they are motivated to do what is right for their children, and they seek understanding and communication with their children. Like all parents, they have desires for self-fulfillment as well as aspirations and concern for their children. In terms of their feelings about education, most parents share certain characteristics:

- They want educators to like children and to command respect of both children and adults. They want their own child to be liked, accepted, and treated as an individual.
- They want to know when things are not going well with their child; they expect honesty from school staff.
- They want to know what goes on in the school and to be involved in classroom activities.

Parents of children with disabilities do have some needs and concerns that differ from those of other parents, although these characteristics are usually differentiated in terms of degree rather than by type. The discovery of the child's handicap and the process of adjusting and helping the child adjust are unknown experiences to the parents of non-disabled children. The strain of caring for a child with a disability and of attempting to plan for that child's future often results in needs for counseling beyond the requirements of other parents. Educational experiences are mandated to be geared to the student's individual characteristics; thus, parents of children with disabilities may feel a greater need for involvement and training than do other parents.

Considering the needs of parents of children with disabilities, school counselors are faced with a challenge and an opportunity to design and carry out a program for parents that is both individualized and comprehensive. In order to develop a successful program, the counselor must examine his or her own attitudes, skills, and knowledge in several areas. Some topics for consideration include the following:

- What are the counselor's responsibilities in working with parents of students with disabilities?
- What counselor characteristics and attitudes are most conducive to the development of positive relationships and sound parental involvement programs?
- What do counselors need to understand about parental reactions to their child's disability and the effects of parental adjustment on the parent-child relationship?
- How can the counselor insure good communication with parents of children with disabilities?
- What specific methodologies for parental involvement can be adapted for use with parents of handicapped children?

UNDERSTANDING PARENTAL CONCERNS

Few parents expect to produce a child with a disability. Although many mothers recount moments of worry—or even panic—concerning the health and physical condition of their unborn babies, those moments are usually fleeting. Thus, when parents first discover that their child is disabled, their reactions almost always involve shock and fear. Parental reactions are too often reinforced by callous remarks or evasion of the issue from medical personnel.

The frustrating experiences that parents of children with disabilities have undergone in their search for diagnosis, understanding, and treatment of their children's disability has led, in many cases, to distrust and suspicion of all helping professionals. The counselor's awareness of such experiences and empathy with parental concerns is a necessary first step in building bonds of trust and communication.

Parental Adjustment to a Child's Disability

Even when parents have not experienced frustrating or hurtful encounters with professionals in their attempts to identify and deal with their children's problems, most parents undergo a painful process of adjustment to the situation. The various stages that parents experience have often been compared to the process of mourning associated with death (Kubler-Ross, 1975) and with the adjustment process experienced by most adventitiously disabled people.

In the first stage, parents generally experience feelings of shock or numbness. Even though the parent may have long suspected a problem with the child, a reaction of acute anxiety typically follows when the difficulty is openly acknowledged. During this period, parents may not be able to perceive clearly or to retain crucial information. They may respond by denying factual information, hoping against hope that the professionals are wrong.

As the numbness begins to fade, feelings of guilt and self-recrimination often follow. The guilt that most parents experience concerning their children with disabilities may be identified with a specific behavior or thought:

- "I should have followed my diet more carefully when I was pregnant."
- "If I had taken him to the doctor earlier, he could probably have been cured."

- "We didn't want a baby and now we're being punished for those feelings."

Under certain conditions, the guilt reactions of parents may be therapeutic. Guilt can serve as a release from the initial reaction of shock and intense anxiety. It is therapeutic, however, only if it is temporary. As parents gain and are able to assimilate more information about their child's condition, they must be able to absolve themselves of guilt and feelings of responsibility if they are to move forward. The parent who remains in a stage of guilt reaction is unlikely to separate from the child or to enable the child to develop to the fullest of his or her capabilities.

A second stage that parents of children with disabilities frequently experience is that of denial or rejection of the diagnosis or prognosis. It is during this period that parents most frequently engage in *shopping* behavior in their desperate search for a more positive diagnosis, for a cure, or even for the most appropriate form of treatment. At its worst, denial of the fact can be extremely debilitating for the family, both emotionally and financially. Moreover, parents are too often continually frustrated by differing opinions, gaps in medical knowledge, impersonal attitudes of professionals, and bureaucratic entanglements.

In spite of the potential dangers of continued or prolonged denial, it also has a therapeutic purpose. The period of denial can serve as a buffer between the initial time of acute anxiety and the stage of acceptance of the inevitable. During the period of denial, hope remains high, providing parents with the drive and emotional energy to seek information and treatment for their child. Denial is an effective defense mechanism, protecting parents from a barrage of emotions that many can only absorb over time.

For some parents, the stage of denial is accompanied by physical or emotional withdrawal. The retreat may serve as a further buffer against the world and its expectations of them as parents. It may be a period in which the family draws together to grieve and plan its future course. For some, the period of withdrawal provides a chance to reexamine the family goals and priorities, and it results in a firmer foundation.

Ultimately, time and the necessity to make decisions force the parents into a stage of **resolution** or **acceptance**. Decisions are made regarding the nature of the restructuring of the family. Parents determine—overtly or unconsciously—how they will interact with the child and with each other; they determine how they will cope with siblings, relatives, and the world at large. The attitudes of the family that emerge at this final stage can form the way in which the child decides to face life in all the years ahead. If the family unit remains strong and a firm foundation is built, the prognosis for the emotional development of the child is good.

It is important to realize that while most parents of children with disabilities progress through the stages described previously, the progression differs in intensity, time, and sequence with each individual. Some parents may have difficulty reaching acceptance of their child's disability because of their own personality conflicts; often, mothers and fathers become stuck in different stages, producing further difficulties. Some parents are able to reach acceptance more quickly, but they may vacillate between acceptance and depression for some time (Johnson, 1991).

Communicating with Parents

No matter what functions the counselor assumes with parents, accurate and empathic communication will be a key determinant of success. Communication is the foundation for all human interaction, and all cooperative action is contingent upon effective communication. Interpersonal communication refers to verbal and nonverbal messages that are designed to evoke a response in another person; it is a complex process in which everyone receives, sends, interprets, and infers at the same time (Johnson & Johnson, 1991, p. 106).

Numerous training programs or models have been developed as guides to the development of communication skills. It is vital to the work of the counselor that these skills be mastered. However, working with parents of handicapped students may require additional communication skills in order to build a trusting partnership. Many parents of children with disabilities are angry because they have received little assistance from the helping professions. They are frequently still in awe of specialists and intimidated by their expertise and jargon. The negative alternatives of constant home care or institutionalization often make parents unduly grateful and humble toward school personnel for accepting their children into educational programs. Parents of children with disabilities have received so many mixed messages regarding proper treatment that they frequently demonstrate a certain indifference to the latest special education approach. Continuing to do what they think best for the child in the face of frequently changing professional advice has resulted in the characterization of many parents as apathetic. In truth, parents of children with disabilities are often exhausted. They have founded parent groups, held fundraising events for their schools, and lobbied for legislation for children with disabilities, while raising their children with the extra demands on energy and time required. The scars accumulating from their many experiences have served only to further erode communication between parents and professionals.

Counselors can facilitate the communication process by following some simple guidelines:

- **Involve parents in every procedure and decision concerning the child.** An ongoing dialogue and a working partnership with the parents will facilitate all efforts on behalf of the student. Help the parents to see themselves as the primary helpers and decision makers for their children, and encourage them to be treated as such.
- **Give parents realistic suggestions (not commandments!) for how to manage their child on a day-to-day basis.** Consider the needs of the student, the capacities of the family, and the resources of the community.
- **Become informed about community resources and relay this information to parents.** Give parents concrete information concerning contact people, advantages, and limitations of specific services and ways to contact appropriate resources.
- **Give copies of reports to parents.** They will need to digest the information, share them with other professionals, and use the information to avoid lengthy delays in obtaining related services. Encourage parents to keep records, with notations of dates, names, recommendations made, and questions asked. Documentation is an important tool for parents of children with disabilities to insure that their child obtains needed services.
- **Be sure that the parent understands the child's abilities and assets as well as disabilities and deficiencies.** What the child **can** do is more important than what he or she **cannot** do, and the parent must be able to help the child develop self-confidence and self-respect.
- **Be honest with parents concerning service deficiencies.** Encourage parents to be assertive in their search for services and stress the child's right to such services.

The strategies or vehicles available for counselor-parent communication are numerous. Written messages, telephone calls, interviews, and formal reports can all be effective techniques if their use is based upon careful planning. The responsibility for parent communication lies with the school, not the parent; likewise, the means selected for communication should be based on potential effectiveness rather than convenience or expediency. Generally speaking, conferences or interviews can be the most effective way of establishing ongoing dialogue with parents. Counselors will often need to combat stereotypical views that conferences are necessary only when problems arise. Many parents hold negative perceptions of schools; counselors can help allay fears and negative attitudes by their own welcoming response to the parents and reassurance that the focus of communication will be on mutual learning. Frequently scheduled conferences, accompanied by materials for the parent (copies of the child's work, examples of school projects, snapshots taken during school activities) can increase the probability of parental attendance at future meetings.

Written communications are usually not as effective as personal contact, but they are appropriate in some instances. Progress reports can be helpful if they go beyond the traditional reporting of grades to include descriptive data regarding the student's progress toward the attainment of specific objectives and qualitative information concerning the child's personal development. Other written communication, such as letters, can be helpful if it is prepared in a professional format. All written communication is more likely to receive the parent's attention if it is sent through the mail rather than carried home by students.

Telephone calls, the most frequently used mechanism for parent communication, is, unfortunately, the least effective. There is no way to insure that the time of the call is convenient for parents, and an unexpected call precludes the parents' preparation for the conversation. Since telephone calls are advantageous only by their expediency, they are poor substitutes for personal interviews. In general, telephone calls should be reserved for making appointments and reporting emergency situations.

THE COUNSELOR'S ROLE WITH PARENTS

It is clear that a comprehensive program of educational services for students with disabilities cannot exist without considerable input and involvement of parents. Within the school setting, all professional staff—administrators, regular classroom teachers, counselors, special education teachers, psychologists, and others—must share responsibility for meeting the needs of parents and involving them in the educational experiences of their children. Within this structure, the counselor's role is pivotal. Whereas other professionals' responsibilities are fairly narrowly and clearly defined, counselors are frequently called upon to conduct a wide variety of activities and to coordinate the efforts of other professionals as well.

The counselor's work with parents of disabled children involves a heavy emphasis on information giving and receiving. The counselor must assume responsibility for conveying a wide array of information that parents need in order to help their children and themselves; likewise, the counselor will need to obtain much information from parents in order to facilitate the educational process. Parents of children with disabilities often require more help than other parents in understanding and clarifying their own attitudes, ideas, and feelings regarding themselves, their children, and the nature of the relationship with their children. Parents of children with disabilities often need help in exploring their own attitudes and feelings concerning the child's disability. Ambivalent responses to their children are too often treated harshly by professionals who cannot understand the tension and difficulties that many parents face on a continual basis.

Another area in which the needs of parents of students with disabilities may differ from others concerns their actual involvement in ongoing educational activities. Parental involvement in the school through volunteer work is helpful for all students, but for children with disabilities it is especially important. Through classroom observation, tutoring, and participation in small group activities, parents of students with disabilities have an opportunity to view their children in an essentially competitive environment. They can gain knowledge of the child's learning strengths and weaknesses, observe the youngster interacting with peers and adults, and learn ways to reinforce learning principles at home. At the same time, the parents' interest, concern, and abilities can be seen by school personnel, a situation that can lead to more positive communication and establish the parents' credibility as active participants in the learning process.

Counselor Attitudes and Behaviors

The role of the counselor is wide-ranging. As with all parents, the counselor should function as a consultant regarding the educational and social needs of the child. In addition, the counselor has a responsibility to provide parents of children with disabilities with information, to facilitate positive relationships with children, to help parents cope with their own attitudes regarding their child's disability, and to assist parents in becoming directly involved with their children's educational experiences.

In order to effectively fulfill the various roles with parents of handicapped students, the counselor should approach the relationship with attitudes and qualities that are conducive to positive and productive interaction. One of the most important attitudes concerns the willingness to accept one's own limitations. The field of special education is so broad that no professional can expect to be well versed in all areas of disability or in the many facets of the educational or therapeutic process. No one counselor can relate positively with every individual. Neither can one be expected to be able to fully understand the frustrations, fears, and constant pressures that some parents face. However, within certain parameters, the counselor **must** be able to empathize with parents of handicapped children in order to respond to their needs. The ability to identify with others, to see the world from another's vantage point, is a basic characteristic of all helping relationships. As Rogers (1961, p. 56) expressed it, "The optimal helping relationship is the kind of relationship created by a person who is psychologically mature. Or, to put it another way, the degree to which I can create relationships which facilitate the growth of others as separate persons is a measure of the growth I have achieved in myself."

Basic to the role with parents is an attitude of the counselor as a co-learner rather than as a teacher. While work with parents of handicapped children will undoubtedly offer many opportunities for the counselor to teach skills or to impart information, the overall structure of the relationship must be based on mutual sharing and learning. Only in an environment in which parents are encouraged to call upon their own resources and reservoirs of strength can important learning endure. In viewing the parents as co-learners and co-helpers, the counselor will often be called upon to demonstrate his or her own inner strengths. The counselor must be able to respect parents who represent a wide variety of backgrounds and diverse styles of communicating and relating to their children. While it is natural to be able to relate effectively with people who are similar in interests, educational levels, and socioeconomic status, the counselor must often look below such surface characteristics to find common meeting ground with parents of handicapped children. Little will be accomplished if the parent feels alienated from or rejected by the counselor because of differences in life-style or values. Likewise, the counselor must be able to cope appropriately with parents who appear aggressive in their demands for answers or with those who are withdrawn, apathetic, and seemingly uninvolved with their children.

A Model for Counselor/Parent Communication

Taking into consideration the needs of parents and the skills of counselors, a paradigm can be constructed that illustrates the various functions that counselors perform with parents. The paradigm is presented in Table 8-1.

Table 8-1
A Model For Counselor/Parent Communication

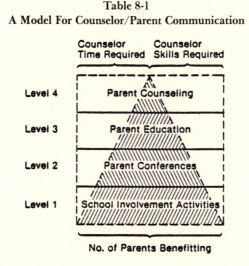

The central section, the pyramid, represents the relative number of parents in need of a given service. The left triangle depicts the amount of counselor time required to implement the intervention. The right triangle illustrates the level of counseling skills required by the counselor in order to carry out the program.

School involvement activities represent an area that would be beneficial to a large number of parents of students with disabilities. As shown in the diagram, school involvement activities require relatively little counseling skill and are not extremely time-consuming for the counselor.

On level 2 are **parent conferences,** an activity needed by most parents of students with disabilities. Parent conferences require more counseling skill than do level 1 activities; correspondingly, conferences require more time than do level 1 activities.

Parent education, on level 3, is needed by fewer parents than those activities on levels 1 and 2, although the counseling skills and time required are greater.

At the highest level in terms of counseling skills and time required is **parent counseling.** At the same time, counseling is needed by the smallest number of parents.

In developing a parent involvement program, the counselor should carefully and logically plan and implement activities that are needed by the parents in a given school or community. Many counselors mistakenly assume that the only way to work with parents is to provide counseling for them. Consequently, few parents are reached, while the counselor's resources in terms of skill, time, and emotional involvement are depleted. The vast majority of parents, then, receive virtually no services from the school; this lack of communication and involvement can seriously damage the parent-school relationship and can adversely affect the child's performance as well.

The ideal parent involvement program, of course, would encompass activities at all levels, ranging from developmentally oriented parent volunteer programs to remedial counseling activities. The counselor's role will vary as well, encompassing the coordination of activities, as well as leadership of discussion groups.

SCHOOL INVOLVEMENT ACTIVITIES

Counselors can help parents of students with disabilities feel more comfortable within the school environment and become more involved in the education of their children. If such a goal were reached, many of the difficulties associated with obtaining parental consent for evaluation, encouraging parents to participate actively in IEP meetings, and fostering home-school communication would be resolved. Parent involvement has successfully produced positive outcomes in terms of student development and parent-child communication (Leyser, 1988).

In establishing programs for parents within the school, the counselor must recognize that goals must be varied according to the needs, interests, and capabilities of individual parents. Practical suggestions for developing parent involvement activities include the following:

- **Plan activities that make sense to parents.** Each parent should be able to readily understand the purpose and value of the program, not just in general terms but also in relation to his or her own needs and interests.

- **Provide parents with the information they need.** Recommendations are more likely to be carried out if they are specific and suited to an individual child or situation.
- **Encourage parents to involve themselves in classroom activities.** Assisting with field trips, grading papers, or tutoring individual children can help parents and teachers develop rapport as well as allow parents greater understanding of the educational process.
- **Plan activities in which parents can work cooperatively with other parents.** Often, parents can learn more from each other than they can from the counselor or teacher.
- **Give parents adequate thanks for their contributions and progress.** Positive feedback encourages greater involvement and commitment to the program.

Counselors can initiate and/or coordinate a variety of activities that will allow parents to affiliate with the school, help other parents, and keep in close touch with their own child's educational progress. A parents' council, composed of parents of children with disabilities in the school or district, represents one way that parents can help each other. The function of a parents' council might include serving as an advisory board regarding educational policy for students with disabilities, serving as advocates for improved school and community services, or acting as a coordinating body for the solicitation of parent volunteers for special school projects or classroom activities.

Serving as volunteers or aides in the school can give parents insight into their own children's behavior as well as knowledge of the daily operation of the school. Parents could assist by serving as resource speakers for career development programs, chaperons on field trips, readers for visually handicapped students, or tutors for individual children. Parents who are uncomfortable working directly with children or adults can assist by keeping records, ordering materials, or maintaining a lending library.

Producing a newsletter for students with disabilities and their families represents another way that parents can increase involvement in the school program and facilitate communication. Items to include could be news about a particular child's progress in a given area; ideas for helping children acquire a personal or academic skill; books of interest to parents or students; announcements of local meetings and events; reports of innovative or interesting school programs; news of recent developments, aids, or devices to aid people with specific handicaps; interviews with successful handicapped adults; or descriptions of community resources, agencies, or services.

The role of the counselor in various volunteer activities is twofold. First, the counselor can serve as the coordinator of the various programs. Once a volunteer program is underway, the counselor's monitoring function becomes minimal, and often the daily coordinating functions can be turned over to a paraprofessional. The second function of the counselor is to provide information to parents. As parents develop support groups, establish newsletters, or conduct workshops for themselves, they will need a liaison who can provide the names of books, sources for ordering films, or names of contact persons in local service organizations. The counselor has much to gain both professionally and personally from this role. At the same time, the counselor will need to participate continuously in professional development activities in order to keep up with current information and materials.

PARENT CONFERENCES

Individual conferences with parents of students with disabilities can prove to be one of the most productive methods of increasing school-home communication and helping the child to succeed in both environments. The advantages afforded by the confidentiality, specificity, individualization, and flexibility of the one-to-one conference offer opportunities for helpful interaction, whether the meeting is designed to be exploratory or to solve a particular problem.

In spite of the obvious benefits and opportunities for mutual assistance, however, effective teacher-parent or counselor-parent conferences are probably an exception rather than a rule. Particularly in school-initiated contacts, parents may infer that they have done something wrong, resulting in reactions such as anger, evasiveness, guilt, or helplessness. The counselor, too, has undoubtedly undergone unpleasant encounters with parents and may have learned to avoid such problems by resisting future contact. Thus, the process is circular, resulting in mutual distrust and lack of communication.

The initial parent contact is the most important determinant of ultimate success in working with parents to assist the child. If at all possible, the first contact should be made toward the beginning of the school year, since research indicates that early contact prevents or reduces school-related problems and maximizes appropriate home-school communication.

Conducting parent conferences when problems are not in evidence has numerous advantages. First, it is an excellent means of obtaining information about the child that the counselor can use in contacts with the student. Information concerning physical limitations can help determine the need for special materials or teaching methods. Information on hobbies or likes and dislikes can give clues as to possible reinforcers in the classroom. In addition to obtaining information, the counselor can use the conference to provide parents with information concerning guidance services available, local parental support organizations, and books and pamphlets regarding disabilities.

When problem-solving conferences are necessary, a face-to-face meeting should be sought at the convenience of the parents, even if it involves considerable rearrangement of the counselor's schedule. The obvious willingness of the counselor to accommodate the needs of the parents and address the child's situation will help lower parental anxiety and communicate an attitude of helpfulness on the part of the school (Price and Marsh, 1985).

Problem-solving conferences can prove to be an exciting and rewarding cooperative venture between parents and professionals, particularly if careful attention is given to certain points. First, it is important that the counselor ascertain who **owns** the problem. Often, a teacher or counselor will assume that certain disruptive behavior that occurs at school must also occur at home. Parents are frequently blamed for their child's acting-out or antisocial behavior, although further examination might well reveal that the problem exists only in the classroom. In cases such as these, the parents' support and suggestions may be invaluable as aids in solving what is essentially the **school's** problem.

It is extremely helpful to give parents as accurate a picture as possible concerning problem identification and the intervention plan. Several steps that can facilitate the parent conference include:

- List and define problem behaviors in observable terms.
- Rank the behaviors in priority order and indicate those that appear to need the active involvement of parents.
- Keep an accurate record of the frequency of problem behaviors for a week and graph the data as a visual record for parents.

- Outline a proposed plan of action, including suggestions for both school and home intervention.

The time of problem-solving conferences is a crucial aspect in determining their success; unfortunately, timing is one area in which counselors, teachers, and other professionals often ignore basic principles of behavior. Regularly scheduled conferences provide the counselor and parents with opportunities to implement action and report progress. Additionally, they can prevent the **crisis conference,** a phenomenon that frequently serves only to reinforce negative pupil behavior.

Problem-solving conferences can be used as a vehicle to give parents positive reinforcement; the parents, then, are encouraged to promote their child's positive behavior. Letters and telephone calls regarding a child's progress are reinforcing; if the school's authority figures, such as the principal, become involved to the extent of calling parents, the reinforcement is even stronger.

In spite of the vast amount of literature advocating the full participation of parents in educational decisions concerning their children, recent research indicates that school personnel continue to resist the development of working partnerships with parents of handicapped children (Margolis & Brannigan, 1990). Some of the difficulties involved in parent conferences can be attributed to a lack of training on the part of school personnel; neither counselors nor teachers typically receive either preservice or in-service training in communicating with parents or conducting productive conferences. This lack of preparation and practice becomes apparent in the school personnel's inability to cope with an angry, defensive, or helpless parent. Often, counselors inadvertently seek to cover their own insecurities or meet perceived parental expectations by presenting an authoritarian or **expert** image. Such an attitude precludes the development of a workable parent-counselor conference.

In order to create an environment conducive to collaboration, the counselor needs to view and treat parents as professional child-rearers rather than as clients. Following are some suggestions for making the individual conference a collaborative professional effort:

- **Be prepared for the conference.** Assemble a folder of the student's work, including positive accomplishments. Make notes on specific areas that need to be discussed.
- **Treat parents with dignity.** Don't keep parents waiting beyond the

appointment time; arrange for the meeting to be held in privacy; avoid physical barriers such as desks.

- **Begin the conference with positive comments about the student.** It is important that counselors view the child as an individual rather than as a member of a group. Parents will respond more positively to a counselor who demonstrates caring for the child, regardless of what problems exist.
- **Listen empathically, without judging.** Giving parents an opportunity to freely express their feelings and concerns will help develop trust and pave the way for mutual problem solving. They should not gain the impression that the counselor is negatively evaluating their feelings and thoughts.
- **Ask questions that open rather than delimit a line of inquiry.** Asking closed questions inhibits a parent's contribution to the discussion, subtly places the counselor in a position of authority, and limits the possibilities for exploration.
- **Avoid professional jargon.** Most parents, regardless of their educational level, are not familiar with many education or psychological terms, and their use may be perceived as condescending. At the same time, parents resent being spoken to as though they are children. Use clear, direct language that is appropriate to their educational, social, and cultural background.
- **Stay on the topic.** The focus of the conference should be the child or the parent-child relationship. Avoid making comparisons with the child's brothers, sisters, or classmates; neither should the conference become a counseling session for parents.
- **Keep the child's achievements and problems in perspective.** Emphasize the positive and express performance levels as representative of a given period of time rather than final pronouncements.
- **Provide accurate and useful information.** If the counselor does not have information regarding resources, rehabilitation services, or other areas of need, he or she should say so openly and make efforts to obtain answers for the parents.
- **Inform parents of their rights.** Counselors have a moral and ethical, as well as legal, responsibility to make sure that parents understand their rights under law and local policies.
- **Reinforce parents' interest and assistance in their child's education.** Like all people, parents of children with disabilities respond positively to praise. Many parents are insecure regarding their own

abilities to teach and train their child; positive reinforcement will build self-confidence and increase efforts.

- **Offer suggestions only when asked.** Often, parents can develop their own solutions when afforded an opportunity to explore them through discussion. Self-generated answers are generally more readily accepted than others' advice. When recommendations **are** made, they should be phrased tentatively rather than authoritatively.
- **Help parents develop a plan of action.** In order to follow up with work at home, parents need concrete activities. If possible, give parents a written explanation of procedures to follow.
- **Summarize the discussion and future plans.** Parents need to feel that something specific was accomplished and will be continued. Review actions that the counselor, as well as the parents, will take, and establish a date for a follow-up meeting.
- **Stay in touch with parents.** Keep parents informed of the child's progress through notes and telephone calls, remembering to focus on positive accomplishments.

One final point concerning parent conferences deals with the involvement of the child. In practice, children are rarely included in such meetings and seldom even informed of them. In the case of very young, immature, or severely mentally handicapped children, their inclusion might not be productive, although the students should be informed beforehand. For most children, participation in a parent-counselor conference has several advantages. It encourages the child to assume greater responsibility for his or her own learning, it prevents distorted reports of what transpired, and it allows the child an opportunity to express his or her perception of events.

PARENT EDUCATION PROGRAMS

Parent education programs are usually organized around a single topic, are fairly structured, and are designed to teach specific skills that parents can use in their interactions with their children. Although the atmosphere is generally informal and opportunities for discussion are provided, the counselor often assumes an active and somewhat directive role.

In recent years an increasing number of **packaged** parent education programs have been developed, representing diverse theoretical positions and topics. Although most programs were not designed specifically for parents of children with disabilities, they usually concern topics such as parent-child communication and behavioral management, areas in which many parents of children with disabilities need training.

So many materials for parent education have been developed during the past several years that counselors could become bewildered in their search for appropriate resources. Reviews and/or evaluations can help the counselor select materials that best fit particular needs and theoretical orientations.

Several suggestions to facilitate the process of parent education include the following:

- **Structure groups.** Parents need to understand the purpose and procedures of each session. Structure also enables members to remain on task.
- **Use universalizing and linking to help lower anxiety about sharing problems with others.** The counselor can point out that most parents share common concerns; when a parent does bring up a problem, the counselor can facilitate discussion by pointing out similarities and differences in the comments of group members.
- **Give feedback to help a parent gain insight into how his or her behavior affects the child.** The counselor can facilitate the feedback process by discussing its function, modeling the process, and encouraging other members to respond on an affective level to a parent's comments.
- **Use redirecting to maximize group involvement.** When a question or statement requiring discussion is raised, the counselor can redirect the comment by asking for responses from the group. Parents are generally more influenced by dialogue with each other than when conversation is restricted to member and counselor.
- **Ask questions appropriately to foster communication and discussion.** In general, closed questions that can be answered by a **yes** or **no** stifle discussion; open-ended questions, on the other hand, provoke thought and imagination.
- **Provide encouragement and stimulate group members to encourage each other.** Effort and improvement, as well as success, should be reinforced.
- **Use brainstorming to allow parents to offer suggestions regarding a particular problem.** In the brainstorming process, evaluative com-

ments are withheld until all suggestions are made. Then the concerned parent responds to one or two suggestions that appear most
feasible, giving a rationale for the choice.

- **Obtain commitments for action.** At the next session the results can
  be discussed. Successful experiences serve to encourage other group
  members; unsuccessful ones allow the group an opportunity to
  examine the action and gain a better understanding of the principle
  involved.

Parent education is not a solution to all parents' problems. Some
parents are distrustful of groups in general; some who are experiencing
extreme problems with a handicapped child may require more intensive
work than would be available in a group setting. When marital difficulties are involved, parents may prefer the privacy of a one-to-one relationship with the counselor. In spite of obvious limitations, however, parent
education has several advantages (Gaushell & Harper, 1989):

- It is beneficial for parents to realize that they are not the only ones
  with a particular problem. Often a parent of a child with a disability
  feels isolated from other parents.
- Feelings of guilt or anger are often alleviated when they are expressed
  in a group. The realization that other members have similar feelings has a therapeutic effect.
- Parents can share solutions. Knowing that other parents have been
  confronted with a situation similar to their own and have resolved it
  appears to make the proposed solution more attractive.
- More parents can be reached in a group than individually. The
  group procedure is an efficient use of time and frees the counselor
  for more opportunities to work with those who most require individual assistance.

PARENT COUNSELING

Although the primary focus of the school counselor's work with parents is designed to contribute to the personal and educational development of their children, there are occasions in which direct parent
counseling is warranted. In some instances, the emotional difficulties of
parents may be greater than the child's handicap; in all cases, the attitudes of parents will significantly influence the attitudes that children
develop toward their own disability. In situations where parental atti-

tudes or emotional stress shows evidence of negatively influencing the development of the child, the counselor can more appropriately intervene by suggesting or offering counseling to parents.

Because of time constraints and the high level of skill required for individual or family therapy, in many instances the appropriate procedure will be for the counselor to refer parents to a community or private mental health agency. There are occasions and situations, however, when the school counselor may feel able to provide direct counseling to parents.

A need for counseling is apparent when a parent indicates that the responsibility of caring for a child with a disability is such that the joy of living is dissipating. The parents of the child may become increasingly unsure of their ability to assume responsibility; they respond by withdrawing from the inner circle of the family but continue to feel guilt about their rejection. Insecure parents need moral support and concrete suggestions for coping with their children in order to be able to assume the responsibilities that are rightfully theirs.

Some parents may communicate their need for counseling through their despair and comments to the effect that "It's a lost cause." Such parents have usually experienced so much frustration and disappointment in their efforts with their child that they are incapable of sustaining further emotional stress. The counselor can help hopeless parents by empathizing with their despair while turning the focus to realistic but hopeful facts concerning the child's potential. It is vital that the counselor not deviate from the truth, but at the same time, he or she should help the parents look with optimism toward the future.

Some parents communicate their need for counseling by withdrawing into their own world and staying there. They may continuously project blame for the child's condition in an effort to relieve themselves of responsibility for action. Some may say nothing—and do nothing—concerning their child's education and treatment. Others tend to continue to maintain the mantle of guilt that most parents of children with disabilities experience at one time or another. When parents remain fixed in a particular phase or stage of the adjustment process, they are indicating that they cannot cope with the stress entailed in dealing actively and continuously with their child's disability. For such parents, counseling can help them break out of dysfunctional patterns and learn to look at their child's problems from a different vantage point.

There is no single recommended theory or methodology for counseling parents of children with disabilities. The counselor should rely on his or her own training and philosophical orientation and should consider the needs of parents and their particular difficulties. For the school counselor, whose responsibilities are diverse and whose time available for counseling parents limited, working in groups with parents of handicapped children may prove to be the most efficient structure. Group counseling provides important advantages for parents, as well as being expedient for the counselor. A group situation provides a framework in which parents are able to understand and conceptualize the emotions they have long experienced but have been unable to sort out. The participation of other parents in the counseling process provides affirmation that parents are not alone in their feelings. Parents often help one another clarify issues and provide support for each other. Group counseling conducted in an accepting environment can result in catharsis, which can be therapeutic in itself. The key ingredient to productive parent counseling is group interaction. The primary responsibility of the counselor is to facilitate this interaction through modeling acceptance, trust, good listening skills, and on-task behavior. Guidelines for counseling parents in groups include the following:

- Recognize that the leader's knowledge of specific handicaps is secondary to skill in interpersonal communication.
- Avoid using diagnostic labels and encourage group members to speak in descriptive terms regarding their own children.
- Don't monopolize the sessions. Lecturing is not counseling and often serves only to destroy rapport and cohesiveness within the group. The counselor must be willing to relinquish some authority.
- Encourage participation by honoring the contributions of each parent. Return questions to the group for discussion and reinforce group members' support of each other.
- Help those parents who find it difficult to talk in a group by noting their nonverbal behaviors and asking them to verbalize their thoughts. At the same time, the counselor should guard against putting so much pressure on people that their ability to verbalize is further diminished.
- Deal with conflicts among members by acknowledging them but not allowing them to consume the majority of counseling time. Because the primary interest of most parents in the group will be on coping with their children, the counselor must not allow this focus to be cast aside.

• Recognize that change takes place slowly. Parents will often verbal-ize insights long before they begin to alter their behavior, and the counselor must be patient with the process.

When organizing a group of parents for counseling purposes, it is advisable to maintain a balance in terms of interests and experiences of the participants. While it is not necessary to restrict the group in terms of the type of handicap of their children, it is helpful to put parents of children of widely disparate ages in different groups. Parents of elemen-tary age children are likely to experience similar concerns with their children, regardless of the nature of disability. Parents of a 6-year-old blind child, however, are probably undergoing different experiences than the parents of a 16-year-old who is blind.

Regardless of the methodologies or strategies used with parents of handicapped children, the counselor is likely to find that the group participants progress through certain stages in their learning. Typically, when parents first enter group counseling, they are not in touch with their own feelings, nor are they able to communicate effectively with one another. They may treat disabilities or differences as guilt-connected and threatening, while denying responsibility for their own feelings or action. They may deal unrealistically with their own situation and problems, talking in terms of fearful expectations or irrational wishes instead of discussing difficulties in the present context and with a view toward realistic hope. During this first phase of counseling, most parents are in an information-seeking stage. They typically ask direct questions and expect the group leader to provide direct and immediately practical advice on how to cope with their problems. Little discussion occurs between group members until the counselor carefully steers the parents in that direction. When this occurs, the group enters a sharing stage. Helpful suggestions regarding child management are exchanged. A skilled counselor will facilitate discussion that goes beyond the superficial, and gradually a feeling stage will develop. During this period, parents examine their own and others' feelings and attitudes and attempt to relate them to their children's behaviors. A generalization phase follows, a period in which the parents' insight is expanded to include greater members, and the community beyond. If the counseling process con-tinues successfully, a stage of maximal function is reached, a point at which parents have implemented behaviors and attitudes that have increased the mutually nurturant relationship between the child and all family members.

The topics that are discussed in parent groups are extremely diverse, but there do appear to be some common threads indicating the most typical parental concerns. Many parents of children with disabilities are caught up in their own emotional difficulties that have arisen from their experiences with their children and various service providers. Anxiety regarding the child's future, pervasive guilt, and ambivalent feelings toward the child are frequent and recurring emotional experiences that many parents need to explore within the confines of an accepting, supportive group. Parent-child communication represents another frequent topic in counseling groups. Many parents feel frustrated in their attempt to understand and respond to their children in appropriate ways. The behavior problems of their children represent another frequent concern of parents; understanding the dynamics of misbehavior and their influence on the behavior of their children frequently results in better management of the child. Whatever the topics for discussion, group counseling with parents of disabled children serves a number of functions: It helps parents understand and cope with their feelings about their child's problems; it coordinates home and school concerns to develop a more consistent approach; it helps parents understand their child's behavior; and it helps improve communication with their child.

BIBLIOGRAPHY

Abeson, A. & Zettel, J. (1977). The end of the quiet revolution: The Education for All Handicapped Children Act of 1975. *Exceptional Children, 44,* 115–128.

ACES–ASCA. (1966). *Report of the joint committee on the elementary school counselor.* Washington, DC: American Personnel and Guidance Association.

Alves, A. J., & Gottlieb, J. (1986). Teacher interactions with mainstreamed handicapped students and their nonhandicapped peers. *Learning Disability Quarterly, 9,* 77–83.

Amerikaner, M. J., & Omizo, M. M. (1984). Family interaction and learning disabilities. *Journal of Learning Disabilities, 17,* 540–543.

Anderson, M. B., & Iwanicki, E. F. (1984). Teacher motivation and its relationship to burnout. *Educational Administration Quarterly, 20*(2), 94–109.

Axline, V. M. (1976). *Play therapy.* New York: Balantine.

Bak, J. J., Cooper, E.M., Dobroth, K. M., & Siperstein, G. N. (1987). Special class placement as labels: Effects on children's attitudes toward learning handicapped peers. *Exceptional Children, 54*(2), 151–155.

Baker, L. D. (1976). Preparing school counsellors to work with exceptional students. *School Guidance Worker, 32*(1), 5–9.

Bakewell, D., et. al. (1988). *Teacher stress and student achievement for mildly handicapped students.* (Report No. 13.) Minneapolis, Minn.: University of Minnesota Instructional Alternatives Project. (ERIC Documentation Reproduction Service No. ED 304 815.)

Bello, G. A. (1989). Counseling handicapped students: A cognitive approach. *School Counselor, 36,* 298–304.

Berkell, D. E. (1987). Vocational assessment of students with severe handicaps: A review of the literature. *Career Development for Exceptional Individuals, 10,* 61–75.

Bhagat, R. S., & Allie, S. M. (1989). Organizational stress, personal life stress, and symptoms of life strains: An examination of the moderating role of sense of competence. *Journal of Vocational Behavior, 35,* 231–253.

Bickett, L., & Milich, R. (1990). First impressions formed of boys with learning disabilities and attention deficit disorder. *Journal of Learning Disabilities, 23,* 253–259.

Boytim, J. A., & Dickel, C. T. (1988). *Helping the helpers: Teacher support groups.* (ERIC Documentation Reproduction Service No. ED 321 199)

Brissie, J. S., Hoover-Dempsey, K. V., & Bassler, O. C. (1988). Individual, situational contributors to teacher burnout. *Journal of Educational Research, 82,* 106–112.

Brolin, D. E., & Gysbers, N. C. (1989). Career education for students with disabilities. *Journal of Counseling and Development, 68,* 155–159.

Brown v. Board of Education, 347 U.S. 483 (1954).

Brown, W. (1986). Handicapped students as peer tutors. *Academic Therapy, 22,* 75–79.

Bundy, M. L., & Poppen, W. A. (1986). School counselors' effectiveness as consultants: A research review. *Elementary School Guidance and Counseling, 20,* 215–222.

Campbell, M. E., Cull, J. G., & Hardy, R. E. (1986). Disabled persons' attitudes toward disability. *Psychology—A Quarterly Journal of Human Behavior, 23*(2–3), 16–20.

Caplan, G. (1970). *The theory and practice of mental health consultation.* New York: Basic Books.

Center, D. B. (1989, April). *Social maladjustment: An interpretation.* Paper presented at the annual convention of the Council for Exceptional Children, San Francisco.

Chapman, J. W. (1988). Learning disabled children's self-concepts. *Review of Educational Research, 58,* 347–371.

Chubon, R. A. (1985). Career-related needs of school children with severe physical disabilities. *Journal of Counseling and Development, 64,* 47–51.

Coles, G. S. (1987). *The learning mystique: A critical look at "learning disabilities."* New York: Pantheon.

Comas, R. E., Cecil, J. H., & Cecil, C. E. (1987). Using expert opinion to determine professional development needs of school counselors. *School Counselor, 35,* 81–87.

Dixon, J. M. (1983). Attitudinal barriers and strategies for overcoming them. *Journal of Visual Impairment and Blindness, 77,* 290–292.

Edgar, E. (1988). Employment as an outcome for mildly handicapped students: Current status and future directions. *Focus on Exceptional Children, 21*(1), 1–8.

Ehrsten, M. E., & Izzo, M. V. (1988). Special needs youth and adults need a helping hand. *Journal of Career Development, 15,* 53–64.

Eigenbrood, R., & Retish, P. (1988). Work experience employers' attitudes regarding the employability of special education students. *Career Development for Exceptional Individuals, 11,* 15–25.

Ellis, A. (1962). *Reason and emotion in psychotherapy.* New York: Lyle Stuart.

Eydenberg, M. G. (1986). Art therapy for the severe and profound. *Child and Family Behavior Therapy, 8*(2), 1–3.

Fabre, T. R., & Walker, H. M. (1987). Teacher perceptions of the behavioral adjustment of primary grade level handicapped pupils within regular and special education settings. *Remedial and Special Education, 8,*(5), 34–39.

Federal Register, August 23, 1977, pp. 42496–42497.

Fenrick, N. J., & Petersen, T. K. (1984). Developing positive changes in attitudes towards moderately/severely handicapped students through a peer tutoring program. *Education and Training of the Mentally Retarded, 19,* 83–90.

Fiedler, C. R., & Simpson, R. L. (1987). Modifying the attitudes of nonhandicapped high school students toward handicapped peers. *Exceptional Children, 53,* 342–349.

Fleener, F. T. (1987). Learning disabilities and other attributes as factors in delinquent activities among adolescents in a nonurban area. *Psychological Reports, 60,* 327–334.

Florian, V., & Kehat, D. (1987). Changing high school students' attitudes toward disabled people. *Health and Social Work, 12,* 57–63.

Freeby, N., & Madison, C. L. (1989). Children's perceptions of peers with articulation disorders. *Child Study Journal. 19,* 133–144.

Fuchs, D., Fuchs, L. S., Benowitz, S., & Barringer, K. (1987). Norm-referenced tests: Are they valid for use with handicapped students? *Exceptional Children, 54,* 263–271.

Gaushell, W. H., & Harper, D. M. (1989). Using a checksheet with misbehaviors in school: Parent involvement. *School Counselor, 36,* 208–214.

Gellman, W. (1959). Roots of prejudice against the handicapped. *Journal of Rehabilitation, 25*(1), 4–6, 25.

Gerber, P. J. (1977). Awareness of handicapping conditions and sociometric status in an integrated pre-school setting. *Mental Retardation, 15*(3), 24–25.

Glatthorn, A. A. (1990). Cooperative professional development: Facilitating the growth of the special education teacher and the classroom teacher. *Remedial and Special Education, 11*(3), 29–34, 50.

Gloeckler, T., & Simpson, C. (1988). *Exceptional students in regular classrooms.* Mountain View, CA: Mayfield.

Goldstein, H., & Strain, P. S. (1988). Peers as communication intervention agents: Some new strategies and research findings. *Topics in Language Disorders, 9*(1), 44–57.

Green, R. (1989). "Learning to learn" and the family system: New perspectives on underachievement and learning disorders. *Journal of Marital and Family Therapy, 15,* 187–203.

Green, R. (1990). Family communication and children's learning disabilities: Evidence for Coles's theory of interactivity. *Journal of Learning Disabilities, 23,* 145–148.

Gresham, F. M., & Elliott, S. N. (1989). Social skills deficits as a primary learning disability. *Journal of Learning Disabilities, 22,* 120–124.

Grolnick, W. S., & Ryan, R. M. (1990). Self-perceptions, motivation, and adjustment in children with learning disabilities: A multiple group comparison study. *Journal of Learning Disabilities, 23,* 177–184.

Grossman, H. H. (Ed.) (1983). *Classification in mental retardation* (1983 revision). Washington, DC: American Association on Mental Deficiency.

Guidubaldi, J., Perry, J. D., & Walker, M. (1989). Assessment strategies for students with disabilities. *Journal of Counseling and Development, 68,* 160–165.

Halpern, A. S. (1985). Transition: A look at the foundations. *Exceptional Children, 51,* 479–486.

Haring, T. G., Breen, C., Pitts-Conway, V., & Lee, M. (1987). Adolescent peer tutoring and special friend experiences. *Journal of the Association for Persons with Severe Handicaps, 12,* 280–286.

Hebb, D. O. (1946). On the nature of fear. *Psychological Review, 53,* 259–276.

Heider, F. (1958). *The psychology of interpersonal relations.* New York: Wiley.

Hett, G. G., & Davies, A. (1985). *The counsellor as consultant.* (ERIC Documentation Reproduction Service No. ED 262 348)

Hobson v. Hansen. 269 F. Supp. 401 (D.D.C. 1967).

Hock, R. R. (1988). Professional burnout among public school teachers. *Public Personnel Management, 17,* 167–189.

Hohn, R. L. (1985, August). *Mainstreaming handicapped children and its effect on teacher adaptation to stress.* Paper presented at the Annual Convention of the American Psychological Association, Los Angeles, CA.

Humes, C. W., & Suggs, M. M. (1988). Group counseling with persons who are mentally retarded on work-related behaviors. *Journal of Applied Rehabilitation Counseling, 19,* 33–36.

Jaret, K. (1987, March). *Stress intervention using cognitive principles.* Paper presented at the annual meeting of the National Association of School Psychologists, New Orleans.

Jenkins, D. E. (1987). The challenge of the marketplace: Implications for school counselors. *Journal of Career Development, 13,* 57–62.

Johnson, C. L. (1989). Group counseling with blind people: A critical review of the literature. *Journal of Visual Impairment and Blindness, 83,* 202–204.

Johnson, D. L. (1991). Grieving is the pits! *Exceptional Parent,* June 1991, 46–48.

Johnson, D. W., & Johnson, F. P. (1991). *Joining together* (4th ed.). Englewood Cliffs, NJ: Prentice-Hall.

Kahn, R. (1978). Job burnout: Prevention and remedies. *Public Welfare, 36*(2), 6163.

Kanchier, C. (1990). Career education for mentally handicapped adolescents. *Journal of Career Development, 16,* 269–281.

Kavale, K. A. (Ed.) (1988). *Learning disabilities: State of the art and practice.* Boston: College-Hill Press.

Kistner, J. A., & Gatlin, D. (1989). Correlates of peer rejection among children with learning disabilities. *Learning Disability Quarterly, 12,* 133–140.

Knapp, S., & Salend, S. J. (1984). Maintaining teacher adherence in behavioral consultations. *Elementary School Guidance and Counseling, 18,* 287–294.

Koestler, F. A. (1983). Visually impaired women and the world of work: Theme and variations. *Journal of Visual Impairment and Blindness, 77,* 276–277.

Krents, H. (1972). *To race the wind.* New York: Putnam.

Kubler-Ross, E. (1975). *Death: The final stage of growth.* Englewood Cliffs, NJ: Prentice-Hall.

Kurpius, D. (1978). Consultation theory and process: An integrated model. *Personnel and Guidance Journal, 56,* 335–338.

Lass, N. J., Tecca, J. E., & Woodford, C. M. (1987). Teachers' knowledge of, exposure to, and attitudes toward hearing aids and hearing aid wearers. *Language, Speech, and Hearing Services in Schools, 18,* 86–95.

Lasseter, J., Privette, G., Brown, C. C., & Duer, J. (1989). Dance as a treatment approach with a multidisabled child: Implications for school counseling. *School Counselor, 36,* 310–315.

Lebsock, M. S., & DeBlassie, R. R. (1975). The school counselor's role in special education. *Counselor Education and Supervision, 15,* 128–134.

Lenkowsky, R. S. (1987). Bibliotherapy: A review and analysis of the literature. *Journal of Special Education, 21,* 123–132.

Lester, R. A., & Caudill, D. W. (1987). The handicapped worker: Seven myths. *Training and Development Journal, 41*(8), 50–51.

Levinson, E. M. (1986). A vocational evaluation program for handicapped students: Focus on the counselor's role. *Journal of Counseling and Development, 65,* 105–106.

Leyser, Y. (1988). Let's listen to the consumer: The voice of parents of exceptional children. *School Counselor, 35,* 363–369.

Leyser, Y., & Price, S. (1985). Improving attitudes of gifted children toward the handicapped. *Education, 105,* 432–437.

Livneh, H., & Sherwood, A. (1991). Application of personality theories and counseling strategies to clients with physical disabilities. *Journal of Counseling and Development, 69,* 525–538.

Lombana, J. H. (1980). Guidance of handicapped students: Counselor in-service needs. *Counselor Education and Supervision, 19,* 269–275.

Lombana, J. H. (1989). Counseling persons with disabilities: Summary and projections. *Journal of Counseling and Development, 68,* 177–179.

Lombana, J. H. (1992). Learning disabled students and their families: Implications and strategies for counselors. *Journal of Humanistic Education and Development, 30*(4), 189–196.

Lombana, J. H., Pratt, P. A., & Clawson, T. W. (1983). *Modifying children's attitudes toward blind students.* Unpublished manuscript, University of North Florida, Department of Counselor Education, Jacksonville.

Love, H. D., & Walthall, J. E. (1977). *A handbook of medical, educational, and psychological information for teachers of physically handicapped children.* Springfield, IL: Charles C Thomas.

Luftig, R. L. (1989). *Assessment of learners with special needs.* Boston: Allyn & Bacon.

Lusk, P. J. (1985). *Counselor adequacy in special education.* (ERIC Documentation Reproduction Service No. ED 289 096).

Makas, E. (1988). Positive attitudes toward disabled people: Disabled and nondisabled persons' perspectives. *Journal of Social Issues, 44,* 49–61.

Margalit, M. (1984). Leisure activities of learning disabled children as a reflection of their passive life style and prolonged delinquency. *Child Psychiatry and Human Development, 15,* 133–141.

Margolis, H., & Brannigan, G. G. (1990). Strategies for resolving parent-school conflict. *Reading, Writing, and Learning Disabilities, 6,* 1–23.

Margolis, H., & McGettigan, J. (1988). Managing resistance to instructional modifications in mainstreamed environments. *Remedial and Special Education, 9*(4), 15–21.

Martin, R. (1978). Expert and referent power: A framework for understanding and maximizing consultation effectiveness. *Journal of School Psychology, 16,* 49–55.

Mathews, R. M., White, G. W., & Mrdjenovich-Hanks, P. (1990). Using a slide presentation to change attitudes toward people with disabilities and knowledge of independent living services. *Rehabilitation Counseling Bulletin, 33,* 301–306.

Matter, D. E., & Matter, R. M. (1989). If beautiful is good, then ugly must be . . . : Confronting discrimination against the physically unattractive child. *Elementary School Guidance and Counseling, 24,* 146–152.

Mazur, P. J., & Lynch, M. D. (1989). Differential impact of administrative, organizational, and personality factors on teacher burnout. *Teaching and Teacher Education, 5,* 337–353.

McLeod, B. (1985). Real work for real pay. *Psychology Today, 19,* 42–50.

Mills v. Board of Education of District of Columbia, 348 F. Supp. 866 (D. D. C. 1972).

Moores, D. F. (1987). *Educating the deaf: Psychology, principles, and practices* (3rd ed.). Boston: Houghton Mifflin.

Moreno, J. L. (1964). Psychodrama. New York: Beacon House.

Myles, B. S., & Simpson, R. L. (1989). Regular educators' modification preferences for mainstreaming mildly handicapped children. *Journal of Special Education, 22,* 479–491.

Newberry, M. K., & Parrish, T. S. (1987). Enhancement of attitudes toward handicapped children through social interactions. *Journal of Social Psychology, 127,* 59–62.

Omizo, M. M., Hershberger, J. M., & Omizo, S. A. (1988). Teaching children to cope with anger. *Elementary School Guidance and Counseling, 22,* 241–246.

Osterweil, Z. O. (1987). A structured process of problem definition in school consultation. *School Counselor, 34,* 345–352.

Patouillet, R. (1957). Organizing for guidance in the elementary school. *Teachers College Record, 58,* 431–438.

Patterson, J. B., & Witten, B. J. (1987). Myths concerning persons with disabilities. *Journal of Applied Rehabilitation Counseling, 18*(3), 42–44.

Peterson, M. (1986). Work and performance samples for vocational assessment of special students: A critical review. *Career Development for Exceptional Individuals, 9,* 69–76.

Price, B. J., & Marsh, G. E. (1985). Practical suggestions for planning and conducting parent conferences. *Teaching Exceptional Children,* Summer 1985, 274–278.

Public Law 94-142. (1975). *U.S. Statutes at large,* 87, 773–796.

Riordan, R. J., & Wilson, L. S. (1989). Bibliotherapy: Does it work? *Journal of Counseling and Development, 67,* 506–508.

Roberts, A. (1984). Bibliotherapy: A technique for counseling blind people. *Journal of Visual Impairment and Blindness, 78*(5), 197–199.

Roessler, R. (1987). Work, disability, and the future: Promoting employment for people with disabilities. *Journal of Counseling and Development, 66,* 188–190.

Rogers, B. G. (1987, March). *A comparative study of the attitudes of regular education personnel toward mainstreaming handicapped students and variables affecting those attitudes.* Paper presented at the Pan American Conference on Rehabilitation and Special Education, Acapulco, Mexico.

Rogers, C. R. (1961). *On becoming a person.* Boston: Houghton-Mifflin.

Rose, E., Friend, M., & Farnum, M. (1988). Transitional planning for mildly handicapped students: The secondary school counselor's role. *School Counselor, 35,* 275–283.

Rosenthal, R., & Jacobson, L. (1968). *Pygmalian in the classroom: Teacher expectation and pupils' intellectual development.* New York: Holt, Rinehart, & Winston.

Salend, S. J., & Moe, L. (1983). Modifying nonhandicapped students' attitudes toward their handicapped peers through children's literature. *Journal for Special Educators, 19*(3), 22–28.

Salzman, K. P., & Salzman, S. A. (1989, March). *Characteristics of adolescents at risk for psychological dysfunction and school failure.* Paper presented at the annual meeting of the American Educational Research Association, San Francisco.

Sanders, J., & Sanders, R. C. (1987). The use of information to improve pre-service teachers' attitudes toward the handicapped. *College Student Journal, 21,* 300–304.

Schein, E. H. (1978). The role of the consultant: Content expert or process facilitator? *Personnel and Guidance Journal, 56,* 339–343.

Schildroth, A. N. (1986). A look into the future: What will students be like? *Perspectives for Teachers of the Hearing Impaired, 5,* 19–21.

Schwab, R. L., Jackson, S. E., & Schuler, R. S. (1986). Educator burnout: Sources and consequences. *Educational Research Quarterly, 10*(3), 14–30.

Seligman, M. E. P. (1975). *Helplessness: On depression, development, and death.* San Francisco: W. H. Freeman.

Sewall, K. S., & Humes, C. W. (1988). Use of a national data base to assess handicapped students' perceptions of counseling. *School Counselor, 36,* 41–46.

Silverman, F. H., & Klees, J. (1989). Adolescents' attitudes toward peers who wear visible hearing aids. *Journal of Communication Disorders, 22,* 147–150.

Simmons, K. (1987). Adolescent suicide: Second leading death cause. *Journal of the American Medical Association, 257*(24), 3329–3330.

Stevens, R. N., & Allen, R. F. (1984). Strategies for improving attitudes toward handicapped students. *Social Studies, 75*(5), 220–223.

Stone, W. L., & La Greca, A. M. (1990). The social status of children with learning disabilities: A reexamination. *Journal of Learning Disabilities, 23,* 32–37.

Thomas, S. A., Foreman, P. E., & Remenyi, A. G. (1985). The effects of previous contact with physical disability upon Australian children's attitudes toward people with physical disabilities. *International Journal of Rehabilitation Research, 8,* 69–70.

Thorndike, R. L., Hagen, E. P., & Sattler, J. M. (1986). *Stanford-Binet Intelligence Scale* (4th ed.). Chicago: Riverside.

Toro, P. A., Weissberg, R. P., Guare, J., & Liebenstein, N. L. (1990). A comparison of children with and without learning disabilities on social problem-solving skill, school behavior, and family background. *Journal of Learning Disabilities, 23,* 115–120.

Travis, G. (1976). *Chronic illness in children: Its impact on child and family.* Stanford, CA: Stanford University Press.

Tucker, R. L., Shepard, J., & Hurst, J. (1986). Training school counselors to work with students with handicapping conditions. *Counselor Education and Supervision, 26,* 56–60.

Turnbull, A. P., & Schulz, J. B. (1979). *Mainstreaming handicapped students: A guide for the classroom teacher.* Boston: Allyn and Bacon.

Vernon, M., & Andrews, J. F. (1990). *The psychology of deafness.* New York: Longman.

Wallender, J. L., & Hubert, N. C. (1987). Peer social dysfunction in children with developmental disabilities: Empirical basis and a conceptual model. *Clinical Psychology Review, 7*(2), 205–221.

Weinberg, N. (1978). Preschool children's perceptions of orthopedic disability. *Rehabilitation Counseling Bulletin, 21,* 183–189.

West, J. F., & Cannon, G. S. (1988). Essential collaborative consultation competencies for regular and special educators. *Journal of Learning Disabilities, 21,* 56–63.

Wright, L. S., & Stimmel, T. (1984). Perceptions of parents and self among college students reporting learning disabilities. *Exceptional Child, 31,* 203–208.

Wyly, J., & Frusher, S. (1990). Stressors and coping strategies of teachers. *Rural Educator. 11*(2), 29–32.

Wyne, M. D., & Skjei, P. (1970). The counselor and exceptional pupils: A critical review. *Personnel and Guidance Journal, 48,* 828–835.

AUTHOR INDEX

A

Abeson, A., 5, 7
Allen, R. F., 53
Allie, S. M., 141
Alves, A. J., 49
Amerikaner, M. J., 27
Anderson, M. B., 141
Andrews, J. F., 69
Axline, V. M., 79

B

Bak, J. J., 30, 48
Baker, L. D., 5
Bakewell, D., 141
Barringer, K., 107
Bassler, O. C., 141
Bello, G. A., 67
Benowitz, S., 107
Berkell, D. E., 95
Bhagat, R. S., 141
Bickett, L., 48
Boytim, J. A., 145
Brannigan, G. G., 162
Breen, C., 53
Brissie, J. S., 141
Brolin, D. E., 96
Brown, C. C., 78
Brown, W., 53
Bundy, M. L., 125

C

Campbell, M. E., 51
Cannon, G. S., 131
Caplan, G., 128
Caudill, D. W., 96
Cecil, C. E., 125

Cecil, J. H., 125
Center, D. B., 31
Chapman, J. W., 28
Chubon, R. A., 82
Clawson, T. W., 55
Coles, G. S., 27
Comas, R. E., 125
Cooper, E. M., 30, 48
Cull, J. G., 51

D

Davies, A., 126
DeBlassie, R. R., 17
Dickel, C. T., 145
Dixon, J. M., 85
Dobroth, K. M., 30, 48
Duer, J., 78

E

Edgar, E., 91
Ehrsten, M. E., 81, 91, 94
Eigenbrood, R., 96
Elliott, S. N., 27
Ellis, A., 52
Eydenberg, M. G., 86

F

Fabre, T. R., 50
Farnum, M., 101
Fenrick, N. J., 53
Fiedler, C. R., 55
Fleener, F. T., 64
Florian, V., 55
Foreman, P. E., 53
Freeby, N., 48
Friend, M., 101

179

Frusher, S., 141
Fuchs, D., 107
Fuchs, L. S., 107

G

Gatlin, D., 49
Gaushell, W. H., 166
Gellman, W., 50, 51
Gerber, P. J., 48
Glatthorn, A. A., 130, 131
Gloeckler, T., 30
Goldstein, H., 75
Gottlieb, J., 49
Green, R., 27
Gresham, F. M., 27
Grolnick, W. S., 27
Grossman, H. H., 29
Guare, J., 64
Guidubaldi, J., 106
Gysbers, N. C., 96

H

Hagen, E. P., 110
Halpern, A. S., 82
Hardy, R. E., 51
Haring, T. G., 53
Harper, D. M., 166
Hebb, D. O., 50
Heider, F., 50
Hershberger, J. M., 75
Hett, G. G., 126
Hock, R. R., 141
Hohn, R. L., 144
Hoover-Dempsey, K. V., 141
Hubert, N. C., 43
Humes, C. W., 67, 96
Hurst, J., 4

I

Iwanicki, E. F., 141
Izzo, M. V., 81, 91, 94

J

Jackson, S. E., 140
Jacobson, L., 49

Jaret, K., 75
Jenkins, D. E., 83
Johnson, C. L., 68
Johnson, D. L., 152
Johnson, D. W., 152
Johnson, F. P., 152

K

Kahn, R., 140
Kanchier, C., 83, 84
Kavale, K. A., 28
Kehat, D., 55
Kistner, J. A., 49
Klees, J., 48
Knapp, S., 127
Koestler, F. A., 85
Krents, H., 45
Kubler-Ross, E., 24, 150
Kurpius, D., 129

L

LaGreca, A. M., 48
Lass, N. J., 50
Lasseter, J., 78
Lebsock, M. S., 17
Lee, M., 53
Lenkowsky, R. S., 71
Lester, R. A., 96
Levinson, E. M., 81
Leyser, Y., 54, 148, 158
Liebenstein, N. L., 64
Livneh, H., 62
Lombana, J. H., viii, 4, 17, 43, 55
Love, H. D., 37
Luftig, R. L., 110
Lusk, P. J., 18
Lynch, M. D., 141

M

Madison, C. L., 48
Makas, E., 47
Maragalit, M., 64
Margolis, H., 126, 162
Marsh, G. E., 161
Martin, R., 127
Mathews, R. M., 54

SUBJECT INDEX

A

Achievement testing, 111–113
Adaptive Behavioral Scale, 113–114
Adjustment to disability
    age at onset and, 23
    by parents, 24
    process of, 24–25
American School Counselor Association, 125
Americans with Disabilities Act, 81
Art in Counseling, 77–78
Assessment of disabled students
    counselor responsibilities for, 105
    evaluation and, 13
    legal requirements for, 103–104
Association for Counselor Education and
       Supervision, 125
Asthma, 39–40
Attitudes toward disabled people
    behavioral reactions and, 51–52
    changing, 53–55
    composition of, 46–47
    counselor role and, 55–59
    of counselors, 60
    development of, 50–51
    peer and educator, 47–50
Auditory Discrimination Test, 122

B

Behavior Rating Scale, 113
Bibliotherapy, 71–74
    advantages of, 72
    definition of, 71
    guidelines for, 73
    process of, 72–73
Blind Learning Aptitude Test, 111
Blind students (see Visually impaired
      students)

Burnout (see also Stress)
    causes of, 140–142
    counselor role and, 144–145
    preventive measures for, 143–144
    symptoms of, 142

C

Career education
    career and educational placement in, 96
    career assessment as function of, 91–92
    career awareness as function of, 90–91
    counselor role in, 82–83
Career Maturity Inventory (CMI), 92
Cerebral palsy, 37
Classroom modifications
    for hearing impaired students, 137–138
    for learning disabled students, 137
    for physically disabled students, 136–137
    for visually impaired students, 139–140
    general guidelines for, 134–135
Classroom observations, 114
Clawson Work Sample Test, 94
College selection (see also Career education)
    accessibility and, 98–99
    resources to facilitate, 99–101
Columbia Mental Maturity Scale, 110–111
Communication
    attitudes of counselors and, 155–156
    model for, 157–158
    with parents, guidelines for, 153
    with parents, strategies for, 154
Conferences, parent
    importance of initial contact in, 160–
      161
    involvement of children in, 164
    problem-solving, 160–162
    suggestions for counselors regarding,
      161–164

L

Labeling, 22
Learning disabilities
  characteristics associated with, 27–28
  definitions of, 26–27
  terminology associated with, 26
Learning disabled students
  assessment of, 121–122
  classroom modifications for, 137
  counseling needs of, 63–65
Least restrictive environment, 10
Leiter International Performance Scale, 111
Lighthouse for the Blind, 99

M

Mainstreaming
  definition of, 5
  evolution of, 6
  success of, 6–7
Measurement (*see* Assessment)
Mental retardation, 28–31
  definitions of, 29–30
  normalization and, 30
Mentally handicapped students
  assessment of, 123–124
  counseling needs of, 66
  counseling strategies for, 67
  guidelines for counselors of, 66
  vocational needs of, 85
Muscular dystrophy, 37–38

N

Non-discriminatory testing, 116
Norm-referenced tests, 106–107

O

Orthopedically handicapped students (*see also* Physically handicapped students)
  characteristics of, 36–39
  classroom modifications for, 136–137
Otis-Lennon Mental Ability Test, 111

P

Parent counseling (*see also* Counseling)
  advantages of, 170
  group leadership skills for, 168–169
  indications of need for, 166–167
  stages of growth in, 169
Parent education programs
  advantages of, 166
  guidelines for conducting, 165–166
Parent involvement
  advantages of, 148
  suggestions to facilitate, 158–160
Parental adjustment to disability, 150–152
Parental consent, 13
Peabody Individual Achievement Test, 112
Peabody Picture Vocabulary Test-R, 111
Physically disabled students
  assessment of, 122–123
  classroom modifications for, 136–137
  vocational needs of, 88–89
Pictorial Test of Intelligence, 111
Picture Interest Exploration Survey, 92
Play therapy, 78–80
PRG Interest Inventory for the Blind, 92
Public Law 94-142
  accomplishments of, 9
  historical development of, 7–8
  intent of, 9
  parental rights specified in, 11

R

Reading-Free Vocational Interest Inventory, 92–93
Referent power, 127
Referral procedures, 12
Roleplaying, 74–77
  advantages of, 74–75
  process of, 75–76

S

Screening (*see also* Assessment), 12
Sickle-cell anemia, 40–41
Simulation, to change negative attitudes, 54–55
Singer Vocational Evaluation System, 94
Slossen Intelligence Test, 111